Sharing the Lectionary for Lent 1998

A Reflection Book
for Small-Group Faith-Sharing

St. Barnabas Catholic Community
Missionaries of the Precious Blood and Companions
Alameda, California

Resource Publications, Inc.
San Jose, California

Reprint Department
Resource Publications, Inc.
160 E. Virginia Street, #290
San Jose, CA 95112-5876
1-408-286-8505 (voice)
1-408-287-8748 (fax)

ISBN 0-89390-415-5

Printed in the United States of America
02 01 00 99 98 | 5 4 3 2 1

Editorial director: Nick Wagner
Production coordinator: Mike Sagara
Cover design: Alan Villatuya
Production assistant: David Dunlap

Contents

Introduction

Dear friends,

In the name of St. Barnabas Parish and the Missionaries and Companions of the Precious Blood, I invite you to participate in a small faith-sharing group this Lent. Every year, the church sets aside this joyful season to prepare to celebrate the paschal mystery with hearts and minds renewed. This year, Pope John Paul II and the bishops invite us to join with Catholics throughout the world as we prepare together for the Jubilee Year 2000.

At St. Barnabas, our special heritage is the lives and examples of St. Gaspar del Bufalo and Blessed Maria de Mattias. Even before he founded the Missionaries of the Precious Blood in 1815, St. Gaspar gathered people into small groups and associations so that they might support and encourage each other to grow in faith and loving service. The need for these communities of faith is just as essential today. The generous love of God, which we experience in the Blood of Christ, compelled St. Gaspar and compels us to gather people, to enliven existing groups, and to start new ones.

The Gospel for each Sunday forms the heart of these faith-sharing materials. The opening prayer from the Sunday and the responsorial psalm are part of the group's prayer each week. The Seven Offerings, composed by Bishop Francesco Albertini, the founder of the Archconfraternity of the Precious Blood and St. Gaspar's director, is one of the prayer options, as are other prayers adapted from our parish's small-group experience.

In 1998, the Holy Father invites us to reflect on the Holy Spirit and the continued presence of the Holy Spirit in the church. This gift of the Spirit is available to us not only in the Sunday Eucharist but also wherever two or three are gathered in Jesus' name. As we struggle to connect our faith and daily experience, and as we listen to others, we come to appreciate the Spirit's work in us.

As the reading from the First Letter to the Corinthians reminds us on Ash Wednesday, now is the acceptable time, now is the favorable time. This Lent, we hear the story of the prodigal son from the Gospel of Luke. As you engage that story, may you experience the Father's love and the community's rejoicing.

Fr. Jeffrey R. Keyes, CPPS
Pastor of St. Barnabas Parish

PS. Check with your parish to see if your community will be using cycle A readings or cycle C readings. Some communities choose the option of using the cycle A readings when they celebrate the scrutinies with their candidates and catechumens.

In our parish, the small groups reflect on the readings during the week prior to the Sunday celebration. That way, we are all prayerfully prepared for the Sunday Eucharist, actively listening to the readings and the homily. Many delightful conversations with the homilist over coffee and donuts after Sunday Mass have been the result.

Texts and Translations

The Gospel texts in this resource are from the New American Bible (NAB), a translation prepared in the 1960s by Catholic Scripture scholars under the direction of the U.S. bishops. The NAB is the liturgical translation used by the overwhelming majority of Catholic communities in the United States, though there are other translations approved by the Holy See for our liturgy such as the Revised Standard Version and the Jerusalem Bible. (Readings from the *Lectionary for Masses with Children* are from the Contemporary English Version.)

After the NAB was prepared in the 1960s, English-speaking Catholics in the United States began to pay attention to the way the language is used and heard by our contemporaries. Scripture translations that accurately reflect the Hebrew and Greek of the Bible no longer use phrases like "any man," "all men," "brothers," "he who believes in me." The U.S. bishops have been engaged in a dialogue with the Holy See about our needs, and they hope to have approval for a new lectionary before we celebrate the Jubilee Year 2000.

In the meantime, we have decided to use the NAB texts in this resource, as they are the texts most of you will hear on Sundays. As we worked with the texts, we were relieved to see that there is not much exclusive language in the Gospels and psalms for these particular Sundays of Lent. When Jesus quotes Scripture in his conversation with the Tempter on the first Sunday, please be assured that it is all of us, women and men, who do not live on bread alone but on God's word. Inclusivity cuts both ways—when God laments about his people's rebellion in the psalm on the third Sunday, our mothers are not exempt, either! Though the scribes and Pharisees who brought the woman caught in the act of adultery to Jesus may have all been men, Jesus challenges us all, women and men, to set aside accusation, judgment, and stone-casting, and to look to the hardness of our hearts. The faith of Israel, and our faith, is that God surely hears the cry of all the afflicted in the psalm for the fourth Sunday of cycle C. The captives returning to Zion from exile included wives and daughters filled with wonder and rejoicing in the psalm for the fifth Sunday, cycle C.

Similar developments are occurring for the prayers the church composes and translates, such as the prayers from the Sunday liturgy which we invite small groups to use as their opening prayer. We have used the inclusive language in the prayer texts (with permission from the International Committee on English in the Liturgy); the original text is given in brackets in a column to the right of the corresponding line. Listening to diverse feelings and experiences with the language of the sacred texts that we share is part of *Sharing the Lectionary for Lent.*

Small-Group Gatherings and Faith-Sharing Suggested Time-Line

Opening Prayer	5 minutes
The Gospel Text Is Read	5–7 minutes
Silence	5 minutes
A Word or a Phrase	5 minutes
The Passage Is Read a Second Time	5–7 minutes
Silence	5 minutes
I See, I Hear, I Feel	5–10 minutes
The Background Is Read	10 minutes
Faith-Sharing: Individual and Group Process	30 minutes
Discerning an Action Response	5–10 minutes
Closing	5 minutes

There are suggestions made in the text about what to do during the silences. These recommendations present two complementary movements: active listening and dialogue. This pattern can help all of us prepare for the faith-sharing to follow. However, there are no right or wrong things to do during the silences—how you spend them depends on you, the passage, and the Spirit of God dwelling in each of our hearts.

Some Things to Remember

- You are called by God on your own spiritual journey. You are in the best position to determine where God is leading you.

- Respect, honesty, openness, and confidentiality are all important for the growth of the group.

- You are invited to share at the level where you feel comfortable.

- Please wait before sharing a second time until everyone else has had an opportunity.

Acknowledgments

These materials were prepared by Missionaries and Companions of the Precious Blood, Precious Blood Mission House, Alameda, and members of the RENEW Team at St. Barnabas Catholic Community, 1427 Sixth Street, Alameda, CA 94501, under the direction of Reverend Jeffrey R. Keyes, CPPS. Special thanks to Evelyn Henthorn, St. Barnabas RENEW Coordinator, and to Allwyn and Cynthia Carvalho, Raymond Dougherty, Maureen Lahiff, Madelen Lontiong, Erica Rivard, and Femy Visperas.

Background material adapted from *Celebrating the Lectionary,* Resource Publications, 160 E. Virginia Street #290, San Jose, CA 95112. Used with permission. All rights reserved.

1. Into the Desert

Opening Prayer

Leader: In the name of the Father, and of the Son,
and of the Holy Spirit.

All: **Amen.**

Leader: O God, come to our assistance.

All: **Lord, make haste to help us.**

Leader: Glory to the Father, and to the Son,
and to the Holy Spirit.

All: **As it was in the beginning, is now,
and will be forever. Amen.**

Leader: Let us pray.

Lord our God,
you formed us from the clay of the earth   [formed man]
and breathed into us the spirit of life,   [into him]
but we turned from your face and sinned.   [he turned]

In this time of repentance
we call out for your mercy.
Bring us back to you
and to the life your Son won for us
by his death on the cross,
for he lives and reigns for ever and ever.

All: **Amen.**

The Gospel Text Is Read

■ Luke 4:1–13

Jesus, full of the Holy Spirit, returned from the Jordan and was led by the Spirit into the desert for forty days, where he was tempted by the devil. During that time he ate nothing, and at the end of it he was hungry. The devil said to him, "If you are the Son of God, command this stone to turn into bread." Jesus answered him, "Scripture has it, 'Not on bread alone shall man live.'"

Then the devil took him up higher and showed him all the kingdoms of the world in a single instant. He said to him, "I will give you all this power and the glory of these kingdoms; the power has been given to me and I give it to whomever I wish. Prostrate yourself in homage before me, and it shall all be yours." In reply, Jesus said to him, "Scripture has it,

'You shall do homage to the Lord your God; him alone shall you adore.'"

Then the devil led him to Jerusalem, set him on the parapet of the temple, and said to him, "If you are the Son of God, throw yourself down from here, for Scripture has it,

'He will bid his angels watch over you';
and again,

'With their hands they will support you, that you may never stumble on a stone.'"

Jesus said to him in reply, "It also says, 'You shall not put the Lord your God to the test.'"

When the devil had finished all this tempting he left him, to await another opportunity.

Silence

Rest in the presence of what you have just heard, in the presence of Jesus, the living word of God. It is Jesus who is speaking in this passage, speaking to each one of us as individuals.

What does Jesus say? What does he say to you?

This is a time to listen—to listen anew if the passage is familiar. Jesus invites us to listen first with the ears of the heart. To help themselves listen with the ears of the heart, ancient Christians let a word or a short phrase, a single image, completely take hold of them. Let the word or phrase from the text choose you. Repeat it over and over, slowly in your mind and heart. This is not the time to ask theological questions or add anything to the text.

There are no right or wrong choices here. If a phrase does not come into focus after a bit of silence, begin reading the passage to yourself, taking your time. Stop whenever a phrase or image connects with you.

Keep things simple in this silence. Do not try to do too much work.

A Word or a Phrase

After the silence, members mention a word or phrase in the passage that appealed to them or spoke to them.

The Passage Is Read a Second Time

Silence

In this silence you can do a little more work. This is the time to engage Jesus in a conversation. Ask him questions about what you heard. Go somewhere with that word or phrase you heard. Talk to Jesus about it. What did he mean? Why did he say this? What is he asking of you at this time? Occasionally in this silence, repeat the word or phrase from above, slowly, over and over again. Then go back to your part of the conversation. In this way, the word of God is always inserted into the conversation.

I See, I Hear, I Feel

After the silence, mention one thing you think the Lord may be saying to you.

Begin your statement with "I see," "I hear," or "I feel."

The Background Is Read

The story of Jesus' temptations in the wilderness always appears on the First Sunday of Lent. This year it is Luke's turn to tell the story. As with Mark and Matthew, Luke's temptation story follows Jesus' baptism. In all three accounts of Jesus' time in the wilderness, the Spirit, manifest at Jesus' baptism, continues to play a key role. Jesus is led into the wilderness by the Spirit.

In the Gospel of Luke, the temptations take the form of a rabbinic dialogue. The Tempter quotes Psalm 91, Jesus quotes Deuteronomy, back and forth, point by point. But much more than a dialogue is taking place. Jesus is symbolically reliving the history of his people, particularly the wilderness years. He is being tempted just as they were. The tempter tries to get Jesus to doubt his identity as God's son and he tries to entice Jesus into taking a shortcut to the promised land. Unlike the wilderness generation, though, Jesus immediately passes the test. He refuses to doubt or test his relationship with God; he refuses to bypass the cross.

As we hear this story, we are reminded that temptations are always part of the Christian life. Jesus is tempted just as we are. Temptations are neither a punishment nor a sign of sinfulness. If we follow the example of Jesus, temptations are opportunities for growth and a deeper connection with Jesus. As in Jesus' case, temptations force us to focus on what is really important.

It is no accident that the church has us listen to this story as we enter Lent. The forty days in the wilderness clearly recall Israel's forty years in the wilderness and the forty days of Noah's flood. For the church, these extraordinary times of transition in the life of God's people remind us that one of the major purposes of Lent is to accompany the elect and candidates preparing for the Easter sacraments. For the entire community, Lent is a time for asking questions and sorting out our priorities so that we can renew our baptismal commitment at Easter.

Faith-Sharing: Individual and Group Process

The goal of faith-sharing is to discover new connections between this Gospel and your daily life—at home, at work, in your neighborhood, and in your parish. By sharing your experience and listening to the experience of others, our appreciation for Jesus and for each other grows.

In the time your group has together, it will not be possible to explore all of these questions.

Each member of the group is invited to share whatever he or she wishes. It can be a response to one of these questions or it can be a totally different experience that connects with the Gospel. Different members of the group may choose to address different questions.

Just remember that the goal is to share your personal experience and the experience of those close to you, not discuss general topics or theology.

- Describe a situation or experience that has renewed or sustained your faith in times of difficulty and struggle.

- Describe an experience that gave you a deeper understanding of what temptation is.

- What do you want to ask Jesus about his words and actions?

- What insights about living as a disciple of Jesus do you get from his responses to the temptations?

For personal reflection

Discerning an Action Response

What invitations and challenges do you hear? Consider your relationships with members of your family, your friends, people you work with, and those you encounter in your everyday activities. Whom do you need to treat differently? What are you, your family, and your small group called to do? Be sure to select action responses that you can actually begin to carry out.

Here are more concrete questions and ideas that may help you focus your desire to respond to this Gospel.

- Where is the Spirit leading you this Lent?

- How is Jesus challenging you to use the church's Lenten disciplines—prayer, fasting, and almsgiving—in new ways?

- How can you begin to apply your insights in your relationships and the situations you encounter daily, for example, at home, at work, and in your neighborhood? In addition to a concrete action that you can do, look for activities that you can do with others to strengthen your relationships:

  - an activity that you would like to invite family members or friends to do with you

  - an activity that you would like to suggest this group do together

- What virtues does this passage challenge you to develop or strengthen? How will you begin?

Closing

Invitation to Prayer

Leader: Come, Holy Spirit, fill the hearts of your faithful.

All: Kindle in us the fire of your love.

Leader: Send forth your Spirit and we shall be created.

All: And you shall renew the face of the earth.

The Psalm (from Psalm 91)

Antiphon: Be with me, Lord, when I am in trouble.

> You who dwell in the shelter of the Most High,
>   who abide in the shadow of the Almighty,
> Say to the Lord, "My refuge and my fortress,
>   my God, in whom I trust."

No evil shall befall you,
nor shall affliction come near your tent,
For to his angels he has given command about you,
that they guard you in all your ways.

Upon their hands they shall bear you up,
lest you dash your foot against a stone.
You shall tread upon the asp and the viper;
you shall trample down the lion and the dragon.

Because he clings to me, I will deliver him;
I will set him on high because he acknowledges my
name.
He shall call upon me, and I will answer him;
I will be with him in distress;
I will deliver him and glorify him.

Intercessions: Offer intercessions for the church and the world. Use free, spontaneous intercessions; or use The Seven Offerings found in Appendix A; or at the beginning of the evening have group participants write down their prayer needs on a small piece of paper and place them in a bowl in the center of the group. At this time, members draw out one of the petitions and make a prayer of intercession. Then take the paper home and pray for your prayer partner all week.

The Lord's Prayer: Pray together the Our Father.

The Closing Prayer: Pray together a closing prayer from Appendix A.

The Closing Blessing

Leader: May the Lord bless us, protect us from evil,
and bring us to everlasting life.

All: Amen.

Leader: Praise and thanksgiving be evermore to Jesus!

All: Who with his blood has saved us.

All share a sign of peace.

2. This Is My Beloved Son

Opening Prayer

Leader: In the name of the Father, and of the Son,
and of the Holy Spirit.

All: Amen.

Leader: O God, come to our assistance.

All: Lord, make haste to help us.

Leader: Glory to the Father, and to the Son,
and to the Holy Spirit.

**All: As it was in the beginning, is now,
and will be forever. Amen.**

Leader: Let us pray.

Father of light,
in you is found no shadow of change
but only the fullness of life and limitless truth.

Open our hearts to the voice of your Word
and free us from the original darkness
    that shadows our vision.
Restore our sight that we may look upon your Son
who calls us to repentance and a change of heart,
for he lives and reigns with you for ever and ever.

All: Amen.

The Gospel Text Is Read

■ Luke 9:28-36

Jesus took Peter, John and James, and went up onto a mountain to pray. While he was praying, his face changed in appearance and his clothes became dazzlingly white. Suddenly two men were talking with him—Moses and Elijah. They appeared in glory and spoke of his passage which he was about to fulfil in Jerusalem. Peter and those with him had fallen into a deep sleep; but awakening, they saw his glory and likewise saw the two men who were standing with him. When these were leaving, Peter said to Jesus, "Master, how good it is for us to be here. Let us set up three booths, one for you, one for Moses, and one for Elijah." (He did not really know what he was saying.) While he was speaking, a cloud came and overshadowed them, and the disciples grew fearful as the others entered it. Then from the cloud came a voice which said, "This is my Son, my Chosen One. Listen to him." When the voice fell silent, Jesus was there alone. The disciples kept quiet, telling nothing of what they had seen at that time to anyone.

Silence

Rest in the presence of what you have just heard, in the presence of Jesus, the living word of God. It is Jesus who is speaking in this passage, speaking to each one of us as individuals.

What does Jesus say? What does he say to you?

This is a time to listen—to listen anew if the passage is familiar. Jesus invites us to listen first with the ears of the heart. To help themselves listen with the ears of the heart, ancient Christians let a word or a short phrase, a single image, completely take hold of them. Let the word or phrase from the text choose you. Repeat it over and over, slowly in your mind and heart. This is not the time to ask theological questions or add anything to the text.

There are no right or wrong choices here. If a phrase does not come into focus after a bit of silence, begin reading the passage to yourself, taking your time. Stop whenever a phrase or image connects with you.

Keep things simple in this silence. Do not try to do too much work.

A Word or a Phrase

After the silence, members mention a word or phrase in the passage that appealed to them or spoke to them.

The Passage Is Read a Second Time

Silence

In this silence you can do a little more work. This is the time to engage Jesus in a conversation. Ask him questions about what you heard. Go somewhere with that word or phrase you heard. Talk to Jesus about it. What did he mean? Why did he say this? What is he asking of you at this time? Occasionally in this silence, repeat the word or phrase from above, slowly, over and over again. Then go back to your part of the conversation. In this way, the word of God is always inserted into the conversation.

I See, I Hear, I Feel

After the silence, mention one thing you think the Lord may be saying to you.

Begin your statement with "I see," "I hear," or "I feel."

The Background Is Read

By this Sunday, chances are the Lenten commitments we made are already feeling too difficult, too demanding. It would not be the first time such feelings have come up among the followers of Jesus. The first disciples also discovered that following Jesus to Jerusalem was a challenge. Luke's version of the transfiguration, however, emphasizes hope. Luke refers to the "eighth day," to the exodus, and to Jesus' glory—all symbols of the resurrection and of Easter. Through these symbols, Peter, James, John, and Luke's readers are given a glimpse of the resurrection, a taste of the glory that awaits Jesus and us on the other side of the cross.

It is a beautiful vision, filled with light, white robes, Old Testament luminaries, and even a voice from heaven. No wonder Peter wanted to stay. Most of us would have, too. What is important, however, is not the vision but to listen to Jesus, the crucified and now risen Savior.

Faith-Sharing: Individual and Group Process

See pages 8–9 for instructions.

- Which character in this passage do you identify with most? (Among the characters to consider: Jesus, Peter, James, John, Moses, Elijah, the other disciples left at the foot of the mountain, God the Father.) What experience in your life connects you to this character?

- What do you want to ask Jesus about his words and actions?

- Describe an event or a person that has confirmed your faith or helped you deal with doubts.

- Describe an event, a place, or a person that has revealed God's power to you.

- Describe an experience that revealed an entirely new dimension of someone you know, an experience that could not be shared with others.

- What insights about living as a disciple of Jesus do you get from this passage?

For personal reflection

Discerning an Action Response

What invitations and challenges do you hear? Consider your relationships with members of your family, your friends, people you work with, and those you encounter in your everyday activities. Whom do you need to treat differently? What are you, your family, and your small group called to do? Be sure to select action responses that you can actually begin to carry out.

Here are more concrete questions and ideas that may help you focus your desire to respond to this Gospel.

- This Lent, what people, situations, and places do you need to seek out so that God can be revealed to you in new and deeper ways?

- Recall the character in the Gospel passage with whom you identify the most. Think of how your life connects with this character's. Share this connection in a conversation with Jesus and the character in your prayer during the week. If you wish to explore the Gospel from another perspective, choose one or more other characters in the story.

- How can you begin to apply your insights in your relationships and the situations you encounter daily—for example, at home, at work, and in your neighborhood? In addition to a concrete action that you can do, look for activities that you can do with others to strengthen your relationships:

  - an activity that you would like to invite family members or friends to do with you

  - an activity that you would like to suggest this group do together

- What virtues do the characters in this passage challenge you to develop or strengthen? How will you begin?

Closing

Invitation to Prayer

Leader: Come, Holy Spirit, fill the hearts of your faithful.

All: **Kindle in us the fire of your love.**

Leader: Send forth your Spirit and we shall be created.

All: **And you shall renew the face of the earth.**

The Psalm (from Psalm 27)

Antiphon: The Lord is my light and my salvation.

> The Lord is my light and my salvation;
>   whom should I fear?
> The Lord is my life's refuge;
>   of whom should I be afraid?
>
> Hear, O Lord, the sound of my call;
>   have pity on me, and answer me.
> Of you my heart speaks; you my glance seeks.
>
> Your presence, O Lord, I seek.
>   Hide not your face from me;
> Do not in anger repel your servant.
>   You are my helper: cast me not off.
>
> I believe that I shall see the bounty of the Lord
>   in the land of the living.
> Wait for the Lord with courage;
>   be stouthearted, and wait for the Lord.

Intercessions: Offer intercessions for the church and the world. Use free, spontaneous intercession; or use The Seven Offerings found in Appendix A; or at the beginning of the evening have group participants write down their prayer needs on a small piece of paper and place them in a bowl in the center of the group. At this time members draw out one of the petitions and make a prayer of intercession. Then take the paper home and pray for your prayer partner all week.

The Lord's Prayer: Pray together the Our Father.

The Closing Prayer: Pray together a closing prayer from Appendix A.

The Closing Blessing

Leader: May the Lord bless us, protect us from evil,
           and bring us to everlasting life.

All: **Amen.**

Leader: Praise and thanksgiving be evermore to Jesus!

All: **Who with his blood has saved us.**

All share a sign of peace.

3. Repent and Bear Fruit

Opening Prayer

Leader: In the name of the Father, and of the Son,
and of the Holy Spirit.

All: Amen.

Leader: O God, come to our assistance.

All: Lord, make haste to help us.

Leader: Glory to the Father, and to the Son,
and to the Holy Spirit.

**All: As it was in the beginning, is now,
and will be forever. Amen.**

Leader: Let us pray.

God of all compassion, Father of all goodness,
to heal the wounds our sins and selfishness
   bring upon us
you bid us turn to fasting, prayer, and sharing
   with our sisters and brothers   [our brothers]
We acknowledge our sinfulness, our guilt
   is ever before us:
when our weakness causes discouragement,
let your compassion fill us with hope
and lead us through a Lent of repentance
   to the beauty of Easter joy.

Grant this through Christ our Lord.

All: Amen.

The Gospel Text Is Read

■ Luke 13:1–9

At that time some were present who told Jesus about the Galileans whose blood Pilate had mixed with their sacrifices. He said in reply: "Do you think that these Galileans were the greatest sinners in Galilee just because they suffered this? By no means! But I tell you, you will all come to the same end unless you reform. Or take those eighteen who were killed by a falling tower in Siloam. Do you think they were more guilty than anyone else who lived in Jerusalem? Certainly not! But I tell you, you will all come to the same end unless you begin to reform."

Jesus spoke this parable: "A man had a fig tree growing in his vineyard, and he came out looking for fruit on it but did not find any. He said to the vinedresser, 'Look here! For three years now I have come in search of fruit on this fig tree and found none. Cut it down. Why should it clutter up the ground?' In answer, the man said, 'Sir, leave it another year while I hoe around it and manure it; then perhaps it will bear fruit. If not, it shall be cut down.'"

Silence

Rest in the presence of what you have just heard, in the presence of Jesus, the living word of God. It is Jesus who is speaking in this passage, speaking to each one of us as individuals.

What does Jesus say? What does he say to you?

This is a time to listen—to listen anew if the passage is familiar. Jesus invites us to listen first with the ears of the heart. To help themselves listen with the ears of the heart, ancient Christians let a word or a short phrase, a single image, completely take hold of them. Let the word or phrase from the text choose you. Repeat it over and over, slowly in your mind and heart. This is not the time to ask theological questions or add anything to the text.

There are no right or wrong choices here. If a phrase does not come into focus after a bit of silence, begin reading the passage to yourself, taking your time. Stop whenever a phrase or image connects with you.

Keep things simple in this silence. Do not try to do too much work.

A Word or a Phrase

After the silence, members mention a word or phrase in the passage that appealed to them or spoke to them.

The Passage Is Read a Second Time

Silence

In this silence you can do a little more work. This is the time to engage Jesus in a conversation. Ask him questions about what you heard. Go somewhere with that word or phrase you heard. Talk to Jesus about it. What did he mean? Why did he say this? What is he asking of you at this time? Occasionally in this silence, repeat the word or phrase from above, slowly, over and over again. Then go back to your part of the conversation. In this way, the word of God is always inserted into the conversation.

I See, I Hear, I Feel

After the silence, mention one thing you think the Lord may be saying to you.

Begin your statement with "I see," "I hear," or "I feel."

The Background Is Read

This passage consists of two parts: a section of Jesus' teaching and then a parable to drive home his point. Both sections appear only in the Gospel of Luke.

Jesus first mentions two incidents that today would be front-page news. Although we have no historical records, they certainly could have happened. At the time of Jesus, the Romans undertook major construction projects in Galilee (one of which was near Nazareth and probably employed Joseph). Pilate may have massacred a group of revolutionaries when they came to offer sacrifice—such a massacre did happen within the Temple courts during the war of 66-70.

The parable of the fig tree is reminiscent of the story of Jesus cursing the fig tree, a story told by both Mark and Matthew. The fig tree appears several times in the Hebrew Scriptures as an image for the spiritual state of the people—bearing fruit or not, as the people are in right relationship with God and each other or not.

Luke's point is clear. In Jesus, the realm of God is at hand. A whole new world order is about to be inaugurated. But the crowds fail to see the coming crisis. Repent, Jesus warns them. Repent before it's too late. If you don't, you will surely end up just like those revolutionaries. The point of Jesus' preaching is to instill a sense of urgency in his hearers and in us. Jesus takes no delight in death; God does not enjoy the miserable results of our failure to listen.

We must want to change; we must choose to respond to Jesus' urgency. But it is not up to us to move into right relationship with God. Jesus takes the initiative—the gardener willingly offers to nourish the fig tree. There is still time for bearing fruit.

Faith-Sharing: Individual and Group Process

See pages 8–9 for instructions.

- Who has been a "gardener" for you? What did he or she give you that you needed for growth; how has he or she nurtured you?

- Whom have you nurtured when others have been ready to give up on him or her?

- Describe a situation that helped you understand that God does not send suffering as a punishment to individuals or groups.

- Which character in this passage do you identify with most? (Among the characters to consider: those who question Jesus in the first paragraph, the bystanders in the first paragraph, Jesus, the owner of the fig tree, the gardener, the fig tree, the bystanders in the orchard.) What experience in your life connects you to this character?

- What do you want to ask Jesus about his words and actions?

- What insights about living as a disciple of Jesus do you get from this passage?

For personal reflection

Discerning an Action Response

What invitations and challenges do you hear? Consider your relationships with members of your family, your friends, people you work
with, and those you encounter in your everyday activities. Whom do
you need to treat differently? What are you, your family, and your
small group called to do? Be sure to select action responses that you
can actually begin to carry out.

Here are some more concrete questions and ideas that may help
you focus your desire to respond to this Gospel.

- How can you discern the needs of those who turn to you?
  Consider your children, family members, employees or
  co-workers, students, neighbors, and friends.

- What can you do to support others engaged in nurturing, for
  example, parents and caregivers?

- Name a group that people have refused to help because the
  group's suffering was considered its own fault. What can you
  do to support the group?

- Recall the character in the Gospel passage with whom you
  identify the most. Think of how your life connects with this
  character's. Share this connection in a conversation with Jesus
  and the character in your prayer during the week. If you wish to
  explore the Gospel from another perspective, choose one or
  more other characters in the story.

- How can you begin to apply your insights in your relationships and the situations you encounter daily—for example, at home, at work, and in your neighborhood? In addition to a concrete action that you can do, look for activities that you can do with others to strengthen your relationships:

  - an activity that you would like to invite family members or friends to do with you

  - an activity that you would like to suggest this group do together

- What virtues do the characters in this passage challenge you to develop or strengthen? How will you begin?

Closing

Invitation to Prayer

Leader: Come, Holy Spirit, fill the hearts of your faithful.

All: Kindle in us the fire of your love.

Leader: Send forth your Spirit and we shall be created.

All: And you shall renew the face of the earth.

The Psalm (from Psalm 103)

Antiphon: The Lord is kind and merciful.

> Bless the Lord, O my soul;
>   and all my being, bless his holy name.
> Bless the Lord, O my soul,
>   and forget not all his benefits.
>
> He pardons all your iniquities,
>   he heals all your ills.
> He redeems your life from destruction,
>   he crowns you with kindness and compassion.

The Lord secures justice
   and the rights of all the oppressed.
He has made known his ways to Moses,
   and his deeds to the children of Israel.

Merciful and gracious is the Lord,
   slow to anger and abounding in kindness.
For as the heavens are high above the earth,
   so surpassing is his kindness toward those
   who fear him.

Intercessions: Offer intercessions for the church and the world. Use free, spontaneous intercessions; or use The Seven Offerings found in Appendix A; or at the beginning of the evening have group participants write down their prayer needs on a small piece of paper and place them in a bowl in the center of the group. At this time, members draw out one of the petitions and make a prayer of intercession. Then take the paper home and pray for your prayer partner all week.

The Lord's Prayer: Pray together the Our Father.

The Closing Prayer: Pray together a closing prayer from Appendix A.

The Closing Blessing

Leader: May the Lord bless us, protect us from evil,
           and bring us to everlasting life.

All: **Amen.**

Leader: Praise and thanksgiving be evermore to Jesus!

All: **Who with his blood has saved us.**

All share a sign of peace.

4. The Well of Living Water

Opening Prayer

Leader: In the name of the Father, and of the Son,
and of the Holy Spirit.

All: Amen.

Leader: O God, come to our assistance.

All: Lord, make haste to help us.

Leader: Glory to the Father, and to the Son,
and to the Holy Spirit.

**All: As it was in the beginning, is now,
and will be forever. Amen.**

Leader: Let us pray.

God of all compassion, Father of all goodness,
to heal the wounds our sins and selfishness
   bring upon us
you bid us turn to fasting, prayer, and sharing
   with our sisters and brothers   [our brothers]
We acknowledge our sinfulness, our guilt
   is ever before us:
when our weakness causes discouragement,
let your compassion fill us with hope
and lead us through a Lent of repentance
   to the beauty of Easter joy.

Grant this through Christ our Lord.

All: Amen.

The Gospel Text Is Read

■ John 4:5-42

Jesus had to pass through Samaria, and his journey brought him to a Samaritan town named Shechem near the plot of land which Jacob had given to his son Joseph. This was the site of Jacob's well. Jesus, tired from his journey, sat down at the well.

The hour was about noon. When a Samaritan woman came to draw water, Jesus said to her, "Give me a drink." (His disciples had gone off to the town to buy provisions.) The Samaritan woman said to him, "You are a Jew. How can you ask me, a Samaritan and a woman, for a drink?" (Recall that Jews have nothing to do with Samaritans.) Jesus replied:

"If only you recognized God's gift,
and who it is that is asking you for a drink,
you would have asked him instead,
and he would have given you living water."

"Sir," she challenged him, "you don't have a bucket and this well is deep. Where do you expect to get this flowing water? Surely you don't pretend to be greater than our ancestor Jacob, who gave us this well and drank from it with his sons and his flocks?" Jesus replied:

"Everyone who drinks this water
will be thirsty again.
But whoever drinks the water I give him
will never be thirsty;
no, the water I give
shall become a fountain within him,
leaping up to provide eternal life."

The woman said to him, "Give me this water, sir, so that I won't grow thirsty and have to keep coming here to draw water."

He told her, "Go, call your husband, and then come back here." "I have no husband," replied the woman. "You are right in saying that you have no husband!" Jesus exclaimed. "The fact is, you have had five, and the man you are living with now is not your husband. What you said is true enough."

"Sir," answered the woman, "I can see you are a prophet. Our ancestors worshiped on this mountain, but you people claim that Jerusalem is the place where men ought to worship God." Jesus told her:

> "Believe me, woman,
> an hour is coming
> when you will worship the Father
> neither on this mountain
> nor in Jerusalem.
> You people worship what you do not understand,
> while we understand what we worship;
> after all, salvation is from the Jews.
> Yet an hour is coming, and is already here,
> when authentic worshipers
> will worship the Father in Spirit and truth.
> Indeed, it is just such worshipers
> the Father seeks.
> God is Spirit,
> and those who worship him
> must worship in Spirit and truth."

The woman said to him: "I know there is a Messiah coming. (This term means Anointed.) When he comes, he will tell us everything." Jesus replied, "I who speak to you am he."

His disciples, returning at this point, were surprised that Jesus was speaking with a woman. No one put a question, however, such as, "What do you want of him?" or "Why are you talking with her?" The woman then left her water jar and went off into the town. She said to the people: "Come and see someone who told me everything I ever did! Could this not be the Messiah?" With that they set out from the town to meet him.

Meanwhile, the disciples were urging him, "Rabbi, eat something." But he told them:

> "I have food to eat
> of which you do not know."

At this the disciples said to one another, "You do not suppose that anyone has brought him something to eat?" Jesus explained to them:

> "Doing the will of him who sent me
> and bringing his work to completion
> is my food.

Do you not have a saying:
'Four months more
and it will be harvest!'?
Listen to what I say:
Open your eyes and see!
The fields are shining for harvest!
The reaper already collects his wages
and gathers a yield for eternal life,
that sower and reaper may rejoice together.
Here we have the saying verified:
'One man sows; another reaps.'
I sent you to reap
what you had not worked for.
Others have done the labor,
and you have come into their gain."

Many Samaritans from that town believed in him on the strength of the woman's word of testimony: "He told me everything I ever did." The result was that, when these Samaritans came to him, they begged him to stay with them awhile. So he stayed there two days, and through his own spoken word many more came to faith. As they told the woman: "No longer does our faith depend on your story. We have heard for ourselves, and we know that this really is the Savior of the world."

Silence

Rest in the presence of what you have just heard, in the presence of Jesus, the living word of God. It is Jesus who is speaking in this passage, speaking to each one of us as individuals.

What does Jesus say? What does he say to you?

This is a time to listen—to listen anew if the passage is familiar. Jesus invites us to listen first with the ears of the heart. To help themselves listen with the ears of the heart, ancient Christians let a word or a short phrase, a single image, completely take hold of them. Let the word or phrase from the text choose you. Repeat it over and over, slowly in your mind and heart. This is not the time to ask theological questions or add anything to the text.

There are no right or wrong choices here. If a phrase does not come into focus after a bit of silence, begin reading the passage to yourself, taking your time. Stop whenever a phrase or image connects with you.

Keep things simple in this silence. Do not try to do too much work.

A Word or a Phrase

After the silence, members mention a word or phrase in the passage that appealed to them or spoke to them.

The Passage Is Read a Second Time

Silence

In this silence you can do a little more work. This is the time to engage Jesus in a conversation. Ask him questions about what you heard. Go somewhere with that word or phrase you heard. Talk to Jesus about it. What did he mean? Why did he say this? What is he asking of you at this time? Occasionally in this silence, repeat the word or phrase from above, slowly, over and over again. Then go back to your part of the conversation. In this way, the word of God is always inserted into the conversation.

I See, I Hear, I Feel

After the silence, mention one thing you think the Lord may be saying to you.

Begin your statement with "I see," "I hear," or "I feel."

The Background Is Read

What happens at wells? Covenant relationships are initiated. "Please offer your jar that I may drink," says Abraham's servant to a stranger at a well (Gn 24). From the beginning of the chosen people, when Rebekah declares her willingness to be the wife of Isaac, Sarah and Abraham's only son, wells are associated with God's blessing and faithfulness.

Just before the story of the woman at the well, Jesus has been named Bridegroom (Jn 3:29), lest we miss the connection. But now it is not only Israel whose redemption consists of being married by God (as promised in Is 62), it is also Samaria. The Samaritans worshiped according to the five books of Moses and longed for the coming of the Messiah, but in the eyes of the Jewish rabbis and temple authorities, they were ritually impure and idolatrous because they were the descendants of intermarriage among the rural Israelites and people transplanted from five other nations (2 Kgs 17:24).

The story of the woman at the well uses these highly charged Old Testament images of marriage for covenant relationship with God and of marital infidelity—the five husbands—for the worship of idols.

In the season of Lent, the church invites the catechumens and candidates, and all who desire to respond more fully to Jesus' offer of life-giving water, to enter into three great stories that model our gradual awakening to faith. Jesus leads the woman at the well, the man born blind, and Martha (the sister of Lazarus) to deeper levels of understanding and deeper levels of relationship.

The acceptance of the water of faith, done in stages, moves the woman from the margins of the community to the center. Jesus engages the Samaritan woman at the well with a request for water. As their conversation continues, she gradually expresses a fuller understanding of who Jesus is. At first, she addresses Jesus as a "Jew" and then as "Sir." She then addresses Jesus as a prophet. As Jesus continues to reveal himself to her, she comes to see that he is the Messiah.

Jesus is not the only one who questions and challenges in this conversation. The woman takes an active role. The conversation occurs in a public place, but the woman and Jesus are alone, so she is able to respond freely. Jesus respects our questioning and gives us the freedom to engage him.

Finally, the woman becomes a disciple and evangelizer. She gradually accepts the gift of living water from Jesus and shares that source of water with others. Though she is seemingly among the least likely (at least on the surface) to be a model, this woman provides a clear example of faith. Faith is a gift, gradually accepted. For those willing to accept it, it is the source of true life and refreshment and the gateway to intimacy with God.

At the end of this story, the Samaritans hail Jesus as the savior of the world. In Jesus, we are invited into the covenant; in Jesus, God espouses us with unconditional love.

Faith-Sharing: Individual and Group Process

See pages 8–9 for instructions.

- Which character in this passage do you identify with most? (Among the characters to consider: the woman of Samaria, the disciples, Jesus, the people of the town.) What experience in your life connects you to this character?

- Describe an every-day experience in which you found "living water."

- Describe a person who has been an unexpected apostle of the Good News for you. Why did this person initially seem an unlikely messenger? How did your understanding of Jesus change as a result of this experience?

- Describe an experience when you have "reaped what others have sown"—in which you have been part of a successful outcome because others have done the planning and initial work.

- What do you want to ask Jesus about his words and actions?

For personal reflection

Discerning an Action Response

What invitations and challenges do you hear? Consider your relationships with members of your family, your friends, people you work with, and those you encounter in your everyday activities. Whom do you need to treat differently? What are you, your family, and your small group called to do? Be sure to select action responses that you can actually begin to carry out.

Here are more concrete questions and ideas that may help you focus your desire to respond to this Gospel.

- Where are you called to be part of initial sowing, to begin something that will be brought to completion by others, laying a foundation the results of which you may not live to see?

- How are you called to reach out to those "on the fringes," engaging others in gentle dialogue and allowing their questions to challenge your way of seeing things? Think about people with whom you come into contact but to whom you are afraid to talk.

- Recall the character in the Gospel passage with whom you identify most. Think of how your life connects with this character's. Share this connection in a conversation with Jesus and the character in your prayer during the week. If you wish to explore the Gospel from another perspective, choose one or more other characters in the story.

- How can you begin to apply your insights in your relationships and the situations you encounter daily—for example, at home, at work, and in your neighborhood? In addition to a concrete action that you can do, look for activities that you can do with others to strengthen your relationships:

    - an activity that you would like to invite family members or friends to do with you

    - an activity that you would like to suggest this group do together

Closing

Invitation to Prayer

Leader: Come, Holy Spirit, fill the hearts of your faithful.

All: Kindle in us the fire of your love.

Leader: Send forth your Spirit and we shall be created.

All: And you shall renew the face of the earth.

The Psalm (from Psalm 95)

Antiphon: If today you hear his voice,
            harden not your hearts.

> Come, let us joyfully sing to the Lord;
>   let us acclaim the Rock of our salvation.
> Let us greet him with thanksgiving;
>   let us joyfully sing psalms to him.
>
> Come, let us bow down in worship;
>   let us kneel before the Lord who made us.
> For he is our God,
>   and we are the people he shepherds, the flock he guides.
>
> Oh, that today you would hear his voice:
>   "Harden not your hearts as at Meribah,
>   as in the day of Massah in the desert,
> Where your fathers tempted me;
>   they tested me though they had seen my works."

Intercessions: Offer intercessions for the church and the world. Use free, spontaneous intercessions; or use The Seven Offerings found in Appendix A; or at the beginning of the evening have group participants write down their prayer needs on a small piece of paper and place them in a bowl in the center of the group. At this time, members draw out one of the petitions and make a prayer of intercession. Then take the paper home and pray for your prayer partner all week.

The Lord's Prayer: Pray together the Our Father.

The Closing Prayer: Pray together a closing prayer from Appendix A.

The Closing Blessing

Leader: May the Lord bless us, protect us from evil,
and bring us to everlasting life.

All: **Amen.**

Leader: Praise and thanksgiving be evermore to Jesus!

All: Who with his blood has saved us.

All share a sign of peace.

5. The Prodigal Father

Opening Prayer

Leader: In the name of the Father, and of the Son,
and of the Holy Spirit.

All: **Amen.**

Leader: O God, come to our assistance.

All: **Lord, make haste to help us.**

Leader: Glory to the Father, and to the Son,
and to the Holy Spirit.

All: **As it was in the beginning, is now,
and will be forever. Amen.**

Leader: Let us pray.

God our Father,
your Word, Jesus Christ, spoke peace
   to a sinful world
and brought humanity the gift   [brought mankind]
   of reconciliation
by the suffering and death he endured.

Teach us, the people who bear his name,
to follow the example he gave us:
may our faith, hope, and charity
turn hatred to love, conflict to peace,
   death to eternal life.

We ask this through Christ our Lord.

All: **Amen.**

The Gospel Text Is Read

■ Luke 15:1–3,11–32

The tax collectors and the sinners were all gathering around Jesus to hear him, at which the Pharisees and the scribes murmured, "This man welcomes sinners and eats with them." Then he addressed this parable to them: "A man had two sons. The younger of them said to his father, 'Father, give me the share of the estate that is coming to me.' So the father divided up the property. Some days later this younger son collected all his belongings and went off to a distant land, where he squandered his money on dissolute living. After he had spent everything, a great famine broke out in that country and he was in dire need. So he attached himself to one of the propertied class of the place, who sent him to his farm to take care of the pigs. He longed to fill his belly with the husks that were fodder for the pigs, but no one made a move to give him anything. Coming to his senses at last, he said: 'How many hired hands at my father's place have more than enough to eat, while here I am starving! I will break away and return to my father, and say to him, "Father, I have sinned against God and against you; I no longer deserve to be called your son. Treat me like one of your hired hands."' With that he set off for his father's house. While he was still a long way off, his father caught sight of him, and was deeply moved. He ran out to meet him, threw his arms around his neck, and kissed him. The son said to him, 'Father, I have sinned against God and against you; I no longer deserve to be called your son.' The father said to his servants: 'Quick! bring out the finest robe and put it on him; put a ring on his finger and shoes on his feet. Take the fatted calf and kill it. Let us eat and celebrate because this son of mine was dead and has come back to life. He was lost and is found.' The celebration began.

"Meanwhile the elder son was out on the land. As he neared the house on his way home, he heard the sound of music and dancing. He called one of the servants and asked him the reason for the dancing and the music. The servant answered, 'Your brother is home, and your father has killed the fatted calf because he has him back in good health.' The son grew angry at this and would not go in; but his father came out and began to plead with him.

"He said in reply to his father: 'For years now I have slaved for you. I never disobeyed one of your orders, yet you never gave me so much as a kid goat to celebrate with my friends. Then, when this son of yours returns after having gone through your property with loose women, you kill the fatted calf for him.'

"'My son,' replied the father, 'you are with me always, and everything I have is yours. But we had to celebrate and rejoice! This brother of yours was dead, and has come back to life. He was lost, and is found.'"

Silence

Rest in the presence of what you have just heard, in the presence of Jesus, the living word of God. It is Jesus who is speaking in this passage, speaking to each one of us as individuals.

What does Jesus say? What does he say to you?

This is a time to listen—to listen anew if the passage is familiar. Jesus invites us to listen first with the ears of the heart. To help themselves listen with the ears of the heart, ancient Christians let a word or a short phrase, a single image, completely take hold of them. Let the word or phrase from the text choose you. Repeat it over and over, slowly in your mind and heart. This is not the time to ask theological questions or add anything to the text.

There are no right or wrong choices here. If a phrase does not come into focus after a bit of silence, begin reading the passage to yourself, taking your time. Stop whenever a phrase or image connects with you.

Keep things simple in this silence. Do not try to do too much work.

A Word or a Phrase

After the silence, members mention a word or phrase in the passage that appealed to them or spoke to them.

The Passage Is Read a Second Time

Silence

In this silence you can do a little more work. This is the time to engage Jesus in a conversation. Ask him questions about what you heard. Go somewhere with that word or phrase you heard. Talk to Jesus about it. What did he mean? Why did he say this? What is he asking of you at this time? Occasionally in this silence, repeat the word or phrase from above, slowly, over and over again. Then go back to your part of the conversation. In this way, the word of God is always inserted into the conversation.

I See, I Hear, I Feel

After the silence, mention one thing you think the Lord may be saying to you.

Begin your statement with "I see," "I hear," or "I feel."

The Background Is Read

Although Luke is the only evangelist to tell it, the prodigal son is one of the best known and loved of Jesus' parables. It has all the ingredients of a touching family drama. However, like most parables, much more lurks under the surface than we might think at first. In fact, this parable is shocking once we free it from the familiarity we have used to tame it. Take the figure of the father, for instance. If anyone in this story is a prodigal, he is. He gives his younger son that son's part of his estate even though the father still has legal rights to that estate and might need it in his old age. He lets the son take the money and run, with no assurance at all that he will ever see the son again. When the son wastes the entire thing, the father not only welcomes him back home, he throws the son an expensive party.

Clearly we are meant to identify this father with God. But this is some God, letting his son waste his inheritance and then welcoming the wastrel back home. Anyone else who acted like that would be thought crazy, or at best a soft touch and at worse an old fool. That is exactly what the older brother says. For all these years, he has been the dutiful son. Yet the older son had never been given a party. Instead, it is his no-good brother who gets the fatted calf. It is not right, he said. It is not fair. And if we had not read it in the Bible, most of us would have agreed with him, too. That's the shocker, Jesus says. God is indeed just like that prodigal father. The older brother, the Pharisees, and the rest of us who have lived by the rules all our lives may not like it, but that is exactly what God is like. When it comes to mercy and compassion, God is extravagant. When it comes to relationships, God spares no expense. God wants to be friends with everyone, from wayward sons and tax-gatherers to dutiful grown children and Pharisees.

Faith-Sharing: Individual and Group Process

See pages 8–9 for instructions.

- Describe a situation in which you found it difficult to rejoice when someone received great generosity because you felt that he or she didn't deserve it. That is, describe a situation in which you were "the elder son."

- Have you been "the younger son?"

- Have you been "the father?"

- Perhaps there is another character in this passage with whom you strongly identify. (Among the other characters to consider: the mother, the family servants, the family's friends and neighbors, people in the distant country.) What experience in your life connects you to this character?

- What do you want to ask Jesus about this story?

- What insights about God's sense of justice do you get from this story?

For personal reflection

Discerning an Action Response

What invitations and challenges do you hear? Consider your relationships with members of your family, your friends, people you work with, and those you encounter in your everyday activities. Whom do you need to treat differently? What are you, your family, and your small group called to do? Be sure to select action responses that you can actually begin to carry out.

Here are more concrete questions and ideas that may help you focus your desire to respond to this Gospel.

- Think of someone whom you have been taking for granted. How can you let that person know that you love and value him or her?

- In what ways can you and your group reach out to those who have been excluded from the life of the parish or community for something they have done in the past? What has to happen so that they can be included?

- Recall the character in the Gospel passage with whom you identify the most. Think of how your life connects with this character's. Share this connection in a conversation with Jesus and the character in your prayer during the week. If you wish to explore the Gospel from another perspective, choose one or more other characters in the story.

- How can you begin to apply your insights in your relationships and the situations you encounter daily—for example, at home, at work, and in your neighborhood? In addition to a concrete action that you can do, look for activities that you can do with others to strengthen your relationships:

  - an activity that you would like to invite family members or friends to do with you

  - an activity that you would like to suggest this group do together.

- Based on this story, initiate a conversation with someone that restores or strengthens a relationship.

- What virtues do the characters in this passage challenge you to develop or strengthen? How will you begin?

Closing

Invitation to Prayer

Leader: Come, Holy Spirit, fill the hearts of your faithful.

All: Kindle in us the fire of your love.

Leader: Send forth your Spirit and we shall be created.

All: And you shall renew the face of the earth.

The Psalm (from Psalm 34)

Antiphon: Taste and see the goodness of the Lord.

> I will bless the Lord at all times;
> > his praise shall be ever in my mouth.
> Let my soul glory in the Lord;
> > the lowly will hear me and be glad.
>
> Glorify the Lord with me,
> > let us together extol his name.
> I sought the Lord, and he answered me
> > and delivered me from all my fears.

Look to him that you may be radiant with joy,
and your faces may not blush with shame.
When the afflicted man called out, the Lord heard,
and from all his distress he saved him.

Intercessions: Offer intercessions for the church and the world. Use free, spontaneous intercessions; or use The Seven Offerings found in Appendix A; or at the beginning of the evening have group participants write down their prayer needs on a small piece of paper and place them in a bowl in the center of the group. At this time, members draw out one of the petitions and make a prayer of intercession. Then take the paper home and pray for your prayer partner all week.

The Lord's Prayer: Pray together the Our Father.

The Closing Prayer: Pray together a closing prayer from Appendix A.

The Closing Blessing

Leader: May the Lord bless us, protect us from evil,
           and bring us to everlasting life.

All: Amen.

Leader: Praise and thanksgiving be evermore to Jesus!

All: Who with his blood has saved us.

All share a sign of peace.

6. Was Blind but Now I See

Opening Prayer

Leader: In the name of the Father, and of the Son,
and of the Holy Spirit.

All: **Amen.**

Leader: O God, come to our assistance.

All: **Lord, make haste to help us.**

Leader: Glory to the Father, and to the Son,
and to the Holy Spirit.

All: **As it was in the beginning, is now,
and will be forever. Amen.**

Leader: Let us pray.

God our Father,
your Word, Jesus Christ, spoke peace
    to a sinful world
and brought humanity the gift   [brought mankind]
    of reconciliation
by the suffering and death he endured.

Teach us, the people who bear his name,
to follow the example he gave us:
may our faith, hope, and charity
turn hatred to love, conflict to peace,
    death to eternal life.

We ask this through Christ our Lord.

All: **Amen.**

The Gospel Text Is Read

■ John 9:1–41

As Jesus walked along, he saw a man who had been blind from birth. His disciples asked him, "Rabbi, was it his sin or his parents' that caused him to be born blind?" "Neither," answered Jesus:

"It was no sin, either of this man or of his
parents.
Rather, it was to let God's works show
forth in him.
We must do the deeds of him who sent me
while it is day.
The night comes on
when no one can work.
While I am in the world
I am the light of the world."

With that Jesus spat on the ground, made mud with his saliva, and smeared the man's eyes with the mud. Then he told him, "Go, wash in the pool of Siloam." (This name means "One who has been sent.") So the man went off and washed, and came back able to see.

His neighbors and the people who had been accustomed to see him begging began to ask, "Isn't this the fellow who used to sit and beg?" Some were claiming it was he; others maintained it was not but someone who looked like him. The man himself said, "I'm the one, all right." They said to him then, "How were your eyes opened?" He answered: "That man they call Jesus made mud and smeared it on my eyes, telling me to go to Siloam and wash. When I did go and wash, I was able to see." "Where is he?" they asked. He replied, "I have no idea."

Next, they took the man who had been born blind, to the Pharisees. (Note that it was on a sabbath that Jesus had made the mud paste and opened his eyes.) The Pharisees, in turn, began to inquire how he had recovered his sight. He told them, "He put mud on my eyes. I washed it off, and now I can see." This prompted some of the Pharisees to assert, "This man cannot be from God because he does not keep the sabbath." Others objected, "If a man is a sinner, how can he perform signs like these?" They were sharply divided over him. Then they addressed the blind man again: "Since it was your eyes he opened, what do you have to say about him?" "He is a prophet," he replied.

The Jews refused to believe that he had really been born blind and had begun to see, until they summoned the parents of this man who now could see. "Is this your son?" they asked, "and if so, do you attest that he was blind at birth? How do you account for the fact that he now can see?" His parents answered, "We know this is our son, and we know he was blind at birth. But how he can see now, or who opened his eyes, we have no idea. Ask him. He is old enough to speak for himself." (His parents answered in this fashion because they were afraid of the Jews, who had already agreed among themselves that anyone who acknowledged Jesus as the Messiah would be put out of the synagogue. That was why his parents said, "He is of age—ask him.")

A second time they summoned the man who had been born blind and said to him, "Give glory to God! First of all, we know this man is a sinner." "I would not know whether he is a sinner or not," he answered. "I know this much: I was blind before; now I can see." They persisted: "Just what did he do to you? How did he open your eyes?" "I have told you once, but you would not listen to me," he answered them. "Why do you want to hear it all over again? Do not tell me you want to become his disciples too?" They retorted scornfully, "You are the one who is that man's disciple. We are disciples of Moses. We know that God spoke to Moses, but we have no idea where this man comes from." He came back at them: "Well, this is news! You do not know where he comes from, yet he opened my eyes. We know that God does not hear sinners, but that if someone is devout and obeys his will he listens to him. It is unheard of that anyone ever gave sight to a person blind from birth. If this man were not from God, he could never have done such a thing." "What!" they exclaimed, "You are steeped in sin from your birth, and you are giving us lectures?" With that they threw him out bodily.

When Jesus heard of his expulsion, he sought him out and asked him, "Do you believe in the Son of Man?" He answered, "Who is he, sir, that I may believe in him?" "You have seen him," Jesus replied. "He is speaking to you now." ["I do believe, Lord," he said, and bowed down to worship him. Then Jesus said:]

"I came into this world to divide it,

to make the sightless see

and the seeing blind."

Some of the Pharisees around him picked this up, saying, "You are not counting us in with the blind, are you?" To which Jesus replied:

"If you were blind

there would be no sin in that.

'But we see,' you say,

and your sin remains."

Silence

Rest in the presence of what you have just heard, in the presence of Jesus, the living word of God. It is Jesus who is speaking in this passage, speaking to each one of us as individuals.

What does Jesus say? What does he say to you?

This is a time to listen—to listen anew if the passage is familiar. Jesus invites us to listen first with the ears of the heart. To help themselves listen with the ears of the heart, ancient Christians let a word or a short phrase, a single image, completely take hold of them. Let the word or phrase from the text choose you. Repeat it over and over, slowly in your mind and heart. This is not the time to ask theological questions or add anything to the text.

There are no right or wrong choices here. If a phrase does not come into focus after a bit of silence, begin reading the passage to yourself, taking your time. Stop whenever a phrase or image connects with you.

Keep things simple in this silence. Do not try to do too much work.

A Word or a Phrase

After the silence, members mention a word or phrase in the passage that appealed to them or spoke to them.

The Passage Is Read a Second Time

Silence

In this silence you can do a little more work. This is the time to engage Jesus in a conversation. Ask him questions about what you heard. Go somewhere with that word or phrase you heard. Talk to Jesus about it. What did he mean? Why did he say this? What is he asking of you at this time? Occasionally in this silence, repeat the word or phrase from above, slowly, over and over again. Then go back to your part of the conversation. In this way, the word of God is always inserted into the conversation.

I See, I Hear, I Feel

After the silence, mention one thing you think the Lord may be saying to you.

Begin your statement with "I see," "I hear," or "I feel."

The Background Is Read

Reflected in this story of the blind man we see some painful experiences of the later church community. For some time after the death and resurrection of Jesus, Christians who had grown up in the synagogue continued to worship with the Jewish community. They still considered themselves Jews even after they had become Christians. But as the years went by, tensions over their claims that Jesus was the Messiah began to create divisions. Eventually the divisions became a chasm, and the Jewish Christians were expelled from the synagogues. This is underneath the parents' refusal to answer the questions or defend their son.

As the story progresses, the blind man increasingly comes to "see" Jesus, which is John's metaphor for "believe in." Like the Samaritan woman, the man begins at square one with "the man called Jesus." After some questioning by the authorities, the man is ready to call Jesus a prophet. Soon he is testifying that Jesus is from God. By the end of the story, Jesus is his "Lord."

At the same time, the synagogue authorities become increasingly "blind." At first, Jesus is simply "not of God." After a while they begin to call Jesus a "sinner." Soon they are not even sure where Jesus came from. By the end, all that remains is their sin. But such is the way with God's light, John says. You either see it or you do not. For John, there is no middle ground. Jesus is either the light of the world or he is not. And if he is, then everything, literally everything, changes: our lives, our perspective, our loyalties—everything.

Twentieth-century Christians need to keep in mind the context of the Gospel. It is more helpful to consider the ways Christians fail to live in the light than to use John's Gospel to condemn those Jews in Jesus' time who failed to see Jesus. We live in the light of faith through our baptism, yet we may also need to be healed from our blindness. Our journey parallels that of the man born blind. The healing Jesus offers is only the first step. Our response to the healing and our willingness to ask deeper questions is part of our journey toward the light and toward Easter.

In last week's Gospel, the woman at the well started out as an outsider; she came to the well unaccompanied by other women from the town. Through her conversation with Jesus, she moves to the center; relationships are restored. This week, Jesus is the outsider, and the man born blind becomes an outsider through his conversation with Jesus. We, those for whom this story is recounted, know from our faith experience that there will be more to the story than the pain of separation from family and synagogue community. We believe that the man born blind, and we ourselves, will be given new relationships in the community centered on Jesus, a community of sisters and brothers.

Faith-Sharing: Individual and Group Process

See pages 8–9 for instructions.

- Describe a situation in which someone made you aware of a blindness you didn't know you had.

- Describe a situation or relationship in which you saw God's glory revealed through disability or illness.

- Which character in this passage do you identify with most? (Among the characters to consider: the man born blind, Jesus' disciples, the man's parents and their neighbors, a synagogue member witnessing the Pharisees' interrogation of the man.) What experience in your life connects you to this character?

- What do you want to ask Jesus about this story?

For personal reflection

Discerning an Action Response

What invitations and challenges do you hear? Consider your relationships with members of your family, your friends, people you work with, and those you encounter in your everyday activities. Whom do you need to treat differently? What are you, your family, and your small group called to do? Be sure to select action responses that you can actually begin to carry out.

Here are more concrete questions and ideas that may help you focus your desire to respond to this Gospel.

- In your local situation, who have had their misfortunes labeled as punishment? In what ways can you personally work to overcome such estrangement?

- In what ways does this story challenge you to engage members of your parish and neighborhood who have disabilities? How can you do this in a way that acknowledges them as untapped resources, people who have something valuable to share?

- Recall the character in the Gospel passage with whom you identify the most. Think of how your life connects with this character's. Share this connection in a conversation with Jesus and the character in your prayer during the week. If you wish to explore the Gospel from another perspective, choose one or more other characters in the story.

- How can you begin to apply your insights in your relationships and the situations you encounter daily—for example, at home, at work, and in your neighborhood? In addition to a concrete action that you can do, look for activities that you can do with others to strengthen your relationships:

  - an activity that you would like to invite family members or friends to do with you

  - an activity that you would like to suggest this group do together

- What virtues do the characters in this passage challenge you to develop or strengthen? How will you begin?

Closing

Invitation to Prayer

Leader: Come, Holy Spirit, fill the hearts of your faithful.

All: Kindle in us the fire of your love.

Leader: Send forth your Spirit and we shall be created.

All: And you shall renew the face of the earth.

The Psalm (from Psalm 23)

Antiphon: The Lord is my shepherd,
there is nothing I shall want.

The Lord is my shepherd; I shall not want.
In verdant pastures he gives me repose;
Beside restful waters he leads me;
he refreshes my soul.

He guides me in right paths
for his name's sake.
Even though I walk in the dark valley
I fear no evil; for you are at my side
With your rod and your staff
that give me courage.

You spread the table before me
in the sight of my foes;
You anoint my head with oil;
my cup overflows.

Only goodness and kindness follow me
all the days of my life;
And I shall dwell in the house of the Lord
for years to come.

Intercessions: Offer intercessions for the church and the world. Use free, spontaneous intercessions; or use The Seven Offerings found in Appendix A; or at the beginning of the evening have group participants write down their prayer needs on a small piece of paper and place them in a bowl in the center of the group. At this time, members draw out one of the petitions and make a prayer of intercession. Then take the paper home and pray for your prayer partner all week.

The Lord's Prayer: Pray together the Our Father.

The Closing Prayer: Pray together a closing prayer from Appendix A.

The Closing Blessing

Leader: May the Lord bless us, protect us from evil,
and bring us to everlasting life.

All: Amen.

Leader: Praise and thanksgiving be evermore to Jesus!

All: Who with his blood has saved us.

All share a sign of peace.

7. A Lesson on Mercy

Opening Prayer

Leader: In the name of the Father, and of the Son,
and of the Holy Spirit.

All: **Amen.**

Leader: O God, come to our assistance.

All: **Lord, make haste to help us.**

Leader: Glory to the Father, and to the Son,
and to the Holy Spirit.

All: **As it was in the beginning, is now,**
and will be forever. Amen.

Leader: Let us pray.

Father in heaven,
the love of your Son led him to accept
 the suffering of the cross
that his brothers and sisters might glory   [his brothers]
 in new life.
Change our selfishness into self-giving.
Help us to embrace the world you have given us,
that we may transform the darkness of its pain
into the life and joy of Easter.

Grant this through Christ our Lord.

All: **Amen.**

The Gospel Text Is Read

■ John 8:1–11

Jesus went out to the Mount of Olives. At daybreak he reappeared in the temple area; and when the people started coming to him, he sat down and began to teach them. The scribes and the Pharisees led a woman forward who had been caught in adultery. They made her stand there in front of everyone. "Teacher," they said to him, "this woman has been caught in the act of adultery. In the law, Moses ordered such women to be stoned. What do you have to say about the case?" (They were posing this question to trap him, so that they could have something to accuse him of.) Jesus simply bent down and started tracing on the ground with his finger. When they persisted in their questioning, he straightened up and said to them, "Let the man among you who has no sin be the first to cast a stone at her." A second time he bent down and wrote on the ground. Then the audience drifted away one by one, beginning with the elders. This left him alone with the woman, who continued to stand there before him. Jesus finally straightened up again and said to her, "Woman, where did they all disappear to? Has no one condemned you?" "No one, sir," she answered. Jesus said, "Nor do I condemn you. You may go. But from now on, avoid this sin."

Silence

Rest in the presence of what you have just heard, in the presence of Jesus, the living word of God. It is Jesus who is speaking in this passage, speaking to each one of us as individuals.

What does Jesus say? What does he say to you?

This is a time to listen—to listen anew if the passage is familiar. Jesus invites us to listen first with the ears of the heart. To help themselves listen with the ears of the heart, ancient Christians let a word or a short phrase, a single image, completely take hold of them. Let the word or phrase from the text choose you. Repeat it over and over, slowly in your mind and heart. This is not the time to ask theological questions or add anything to the text.

There are no right or wrong choices here. If a phrase does not come into focus after a bit of silence, begin reading the passage to yourself, taking your time. Stop whenever a phrase or image connects with you.

Keep things simple in this silence. Do not try to do too much work.

A Word or a Phrase

After the silence, members mention a word or phrase in the passage that appealed to them or spoke to them.

The Passage Is Read a Second Time

Silence

In this silence you can do a little more work. This is the time to engage Jesus in a conversation. Ask him questions about what you heard. Go somewhere with that word or phrase you heard. Talk to Jesus about it. What did he mean? Why did he say this? What is he asking of you at this time? Occasionally in this silence, repeat the word or phrase from above, slowly, over and over again. Then go back to your part of the conversation. In this way, the word of God is always inserted into the conversation.

I See, I Hear, I Feel

After the silence, mention one thing you think the Lord may be saying to you.

Begin your statement with "I see," "I hear," or "I feel."

The Background Is Read

Jesus is teaching in the temple area. The scribes and Pharisees approach him, bringing a woman they claim has been caught committing adultery. This is an offense for which the Law specified the death penalty; Leviticus 20:10 says "If a man commits adultery with his neighbor's wife, both the adulterer and the adulteress shall be put to death." The Pharisees ask Jesus, "What do you think?"

The real action is in the plot beneath the plot. The Pharisees are really interested in trapping Jesus, not in obedience to the Law. If they were truly seeking to follow the Law, they would have *also* brought the man caught in adultery to Jesus.

Jesus, however, is not interested in legal machinations. Instead, he wants to demonstrate God's forgiving love and the new life that love offers to all who are willing to receive it. He begins with the Pharisees. He very gently, but firmly, holds a mirror before their faces, hoping that when they see themselves they will have more compassion for another just like them. We do not know why the Pharisees leave, whether they truly are in solidarity with the woman or just shamed, but they do leave, so there is no possible question of witnesses. Jesus then speaks to the woman. He says two things to her, both crucial: "Neither do I condemn you" (she is free) and "But from now on, avoid this sin" (she is called to live as a child of God).

Faith-Sharing: Individual and Group Process

See pages 8–9 for instructions.

- Which character in this passage do you identify with most? (Among the characters to consider: the Pharisees, the woman, her partner in adultery, her husband, their children and their relatives, Jesus, the bystanders.) What experience in your life connects you to this character?

- In our time, what individual or group do you believe deserves condemnation for their actions? As you reflect on Jesus' actions in this story, what do you discover about yourself?

- Describe a confrontational situation in which you or someone you know has acted as Jesus did, allowing both accusers and those accused to keep their dignity and "save face."

- What do you want to ask Jesus about his words and actions?

For personal reflection

Discerning an Action Response

What invitations and challenges do you hear? Consider your relationships with members of your family, your friends, people you work with, and those you encounter in your everyday activities. Whom do you need to treat differently? What are you, your family, and your small group called to do? Be sure to select action responses that you can actually begin to carry out.

Here are more concrete questions and ideas that may help you focus your desire to respond to this Gospel.

- In what confrontation situation can you act as Jesus did?

- Recall the character in the Gospel passage with whom you identify the most. Think of how your life connects with this character's. Share this connection in a conversation with Jesus and the character in your prayer during the week. If you wish to explore the Gospel from another perspective, choose one or more other characters in the story.

- How can you begin to apply your insights in your relationships and the situations you encounter daily—for example, at home, at work, and in your neighborhood? In addition to a concrete action that you can do, look for activities that you can do with others to strengthen your relationships:

  - an activity that you would like to invite family members or friends to do with you

- an activity that you would like to suggest this group do together

- Based on Jesus' actions and words in this Gospel, initiate a conversation with someone that restores or strengthens a relationship.

- What virtues do the characters in this passage challenge you to develop or strengthen? How will you begin?

Closing

Invitation to Prayer

Leader: Come, Holy Spirit, fill the hearts of your faithful.

All: Kindle in us the fire of your love.

Leader: Send forth your Spirit and we shall be created.

All: And you shall renew the face of the earth.

The Psalm (from Psalm 126)

Antiphon: The Lord had done great things for us;
we are filled with joy.

When the Lord brought back the captives of Zion,
we were like men dreaming.
Then our mouth was filled with laughter,
and our tongue with rejoicing.

They said among the nations,
"The Lord has done great things for them."
The Lord has done great things for us;
we are glad indeed.

Restore our fortunes, O Lord,
like the torrents in the southern desert.
Those that sow in tears
shall reap rejoicing.

Although they go forth weeping,
  carrying seed to be sown,
They shall come back rejoicing,
  carrying their sheaves.

Intercessions: Offer intercessions for the church and the world. Use free, spontaneous intercessions; or use The Seven Offerings found in Appendix A; or at the beginning of the evening have group participants write down their prayer needs on a small piece of paper and place them in a bowl in the center of the group. At this time, members draw out one of the petitions and make a prayer of intercession. Then take the paper home and pray for your prayer partner all week.

The Lord's Prayer: Pray together the Our Father.

The Closing Prayer: Pray together a closing prayer from Appendix A.

The Closing Blessing

Leader: May the Lord bless us, protect us from evil,
         and bring us to everlasting life.

All: **Amen.**

Leader: Praise and thanksgiving be evermore to Jesus!

All: **Who with his blood has saved us.**

All share a sign of peace.

8. I Am the Resurrection and the Life

Opening Prayer

Leader: In the name of the Father, and of the Son,
and of the Holy Spirit.

All: Amen.

Leader: O God, come to our assistance.

All: Lord, make haste to help us.

Leader: Glory to the Father, and to the Son,
and to the Holy Spirit.

**All: As it was in the beginning, is now,
and will be forever. Amen.**

Leader: Let us pray.

Father in heaven,
the love of your Son led him to accept
   the suffering of the cross
that his brothers and sisters might glory   [his brothers]
   in new life.
Change our selfishness into self-giving.
Help us to embrace the world you have given us,
that we may transform the darkness of its pain
into the life and joy of Easter.

Grant this through Christ our Lord.

All: Amen.

The Gospel Text Is Read

■ John 11:1-45

There was a certain man named Lazarus who was sick. He was from Bethany, the village of Mary and her sister Martha. (This Mary whose brother Lazarus was sick was the one who anointed the Lord with perfume and dried his feet with her hair.) The sisters sent word to Jesus to inform him, "Lord, the one you love is sick." Upon hearing this, Jesus said:

"This sickness is not to end in death;

rather it is for God's glory,

that through it the Son of God may be glorified."

Jesus loved Martha and her sister and Lazarus very much. Yet, after hearing that Lazarus was sick, he stayed on where he was for two days more. Finally he said to his disciples, "Let us go back to Judea." "Rabbi," protested the disciples, "with the Jews only recently trying to stone you, you are going back up there again?" Jesus answered:

"Are there not twelve hours of daylight?

If a man goes walking by day he does not stumble,

because he sees the world bathed in light.

But if he goes walking at night he will stumble,

since there is no light in him."

After uttering these words, he added, "Our beloved Lazarus has fallen asleep, but I am going there to wake him." At this the disciples objected, "Lord, if he is asleep his life will be saved." Jesus had been speaking about his death, but they thought he meant sleep in the sense of slumber. Finally Jesus said plainly, "Lazarus is dead. For your sakes I am glad I was not there, that you may come to believe. In any event, let us go to him." Then Thomas (the name means "Twin") said to his fellow disciples, "Let us go along, to die with him."

When Jesus arrived at Bethany, he found that Lazarus had already been in the tomb four days. The village was not far from Jerusalem—just under two miles—and many Jewish people had come out to console Martha and Mary over their brother. When Martha heard that Jesus was coming she went to meet him, while Mary sat at home. Martha said to Jesus, "Lord, if you had been here, my brother would never have died. Even now, I am sure that God will give you whatever you ask of him." "Your brother will rise again," Jesus assured her. "I know he will rise again," Martha replied, "in the resurrection on the last day." Jesus told her:

"I am the resurrection and the life:

whoever believes in me,

though he should die, will come to life;

and whoever is alive and believes in me will never die.

Do you believe this?" "Yes, Lord," she replied. "I have come to believe that you are the Messiah, the Son of God: he who is to come into the world."

When she had said this she went back and called her sister Mary. "The Teacher is here, asking for you," she whispered. As soon as Mary heard this, she got up and started out in his direction. (Actually Jesus had not yet come into the village but was still at the spot where Martha had met him.) The Jews who were in the house with Mary consoling her saw her get up quickly and go out, so they followed her, thinking she was going to the tomb to weep there. When Mary came to the place where Jesus was, seeing him, she fell at his feet and said to him, "Lord, if you had been here my brother never would have died." When Jesus saw her weeping, and the Jewish folk who had accompanied her also weeping, he was troubled in spirit, moved by the deepest emotions. "Where have you laid him?" he asked. "Lord, come and see," they said. Jesus began to weep, which caused the Jews to remark, "See how much he loved him!" But some said, "He opened the eyes of that blind man. Why could he not have done something to stop this man from dying?" Once again troubled in spirit, Jesus approached the tomb.

It was a cave with a stone laid across it. "Take away the stone," Jesus directed. Martha, the dead man's sister, said to him, "Lord, it has been four days now; surely there will be a stench!" Jesus replied, "Did I not assure you that if you believed you would see the glory of God?" They then took away the stone and Jesus looked upward and said:

"Father, I thank you for having heard me.

I know that you always hear me

but I have said this for the sake of the crowd,

that they may believe that you sent me."

Having said this, he called loudly, "Lazarus, come out!" The dead man came out, bound hand and foot with linen strips, his face wrapped in a cloth. "Untie him," Jesus told them, "and let him go free."

This caused many of the Jews who had come to visit Mary, and had seen what Jesus did, to put their faith in him.

Silence

Rest in the presence of what you have just heard, in the presence of Jesus, the living word of God. It is Jesus who is speaking in this passage, speaking to each one of us as individuals.

What does Jesus say? What does he say to you?

This is a time to listen—to listen anew if the passage is familiar. Jesus invites us to listen first with the ears of the heart. To help themselves listen with the ears of the heart, ancient Christians let a word or a short phrase, a single image, completely take hold of them. Let the word or phrase from the text choose you. Repeat it over and over, slowly in your mind and heart. This is not the time to ask theological questions or add anything to the text.

There are no right or wrong choices here. If a phrase does not come into focus after a bit of silence, begin reading the passage to yourself, taking your time. Stop whenever a phrase or image connects with you.

Keep things simple in this silence. Do not try to do too much work.

A Word or a Phrase

After the silence, members mention a word or phrase in the passage that appealed to them or spoke to them.

The Passage Is Read a Second Time

Silence

In this silence you can do a little more work. This is the time to engage Jesus in a conversation. Ask him questions about what you heard. Go somewhere with that word or phrase you heard. Talk to Jesus about it. What did he mean? Why did he say this? What is he asking of you at this time? Occasionally in this silence, repeat the word or phrase from above, slowly, over and over again. Then go back to your part of the conversation. In this way, the word of God is always inserted into the conversation.

I See, I Hear, I Feel

After the silence, mention one thing you think the Lord may be saying to you.

Begin your statement with "I see," "I hear," or "I feel."

The Background Is Read

All through the Gospel of John, Jesus performs signs which reveal that he is the cosmic "Son sent by the Father." The raising of Lazarus is the last and most significant sign and it points directly to Jesus' passion, his "hour." Such a moment is thick with irony. Jesus, who is the resurrection and the life, stops on his own journey to death in order to raise his friend. It is a fateful decision, for as John tells it, the raising of Lazarus sets in motion the fatal plot against Jesus.

Hints of the passion are everywhere. Jesus says that what has happened to Lazarus happened in order to "glorify the Son," in other words, bring him closer to the cross. Thomas is even more straightforward about the connection. "Let us also go, that we may die with him," he says. The purpose of this sign, and of all the signs, is that those who see it might believe in Jesus and the One who has sent him. Jesus tells the disciples that he delayed going to Lazarus so that the disciples might believe. When Martha says she knows Lazarus will rise in the last days, Jesus tells her that whoever believes in him will not die but live. He then asks her, "Do you believe this?" She says she does, giving the confession of faith that the other Evangelists credit to Peter. Jesus also prays at the tomb so that the people there might believe. Moreover, the people do begin to believe, much to the consternation of the Pharisees and chief priests.

For John, though, the most significant question is the one left unstated. Do we, the readers, believe? Do we down deep in our hearts believe, like Thomas, Martha, Mary, the other disciples, and the crowd, that Jesus is indeed the resurrection and the life? The answer, John says, is indeed a matter of life and death.

Faith-Sharing: Individual and Group Process

See pages 8–9 for instructions.

- How have you experienced "death," having to say good-bye to people or places, ending relationships, failing at projects that were important to you?

- What "resurrection" stories do you have to share? How have you experienced Jesus bringing dead relationships to life—friendships; relationships between sisters and brothers, in-laws, parents and children, husbands and wives; relationships with the church?

- Which character in this passage do you identify with most? (Among the characters to consider: Lazarus, Martha, Mary, the friends of Martha and Mary, the disciples.) What experience in your life connects you to this character?

- In what areas of your life is Jesus calling you forth? What is holding you bound that Jesus can command to be loosed?

- In what ways do you believe our community needs resurrection? What fears accompany opening the tomb? What causes us to hesitate to obey Jesus when he says, "Take away the stone," so that he can call us forth?

For personal reflection

Discerning an Action Response

What invitations and challenges do you hear? Consider your relationships with members of your family, your friends, people you work with, and those you encounter in your everyday activities. Whom do you need to treat differently? What are you, your family, and your small group called to do? Be sure to select action responses that you can actually begin to carry out.

Here are more concrete questions and ideas that may help you focus your desire to respond to this Gospel.

- What can you do to support others who are grieving losses? How can your small group and your parish be more present to those who are grieving?

- In what ways do you hear Jesus inviting us to participate in his work of raising people to life? How is Jesus commanding you to unbind people and let them go free?

- Recall the character in the Gospel passage with whom you identify the most. Think of how your life connects with this character's. Share this connection in a conversation with Jesus and the character in your prayer during the week. If you wish to explore the Gospel from another perspective, choose one or more other characters in the story.

- If you chose the fourth or fifth faith-sharing question, what steps can you take to respond to Jesus and to deal with your fears?

Closing

Invitation to Prayer

Leader: Come, Holy Spirit, fill the hearts of your faithful.

All: Kindle in us the fire of your love.

Leader: Send forth your Spirit and we shall be created.

All: And you shall renew the face of the earth.

The Psalm (from Psalm 130)

Antiphon: With the Lord there is mercy,
    and fullness of redemption.

> Out of the depths I cry to you, O Lord;
>   Lord, hear my voice!
> Let your ears be attentive
>   to my voice in supplication.
>
> If you, O Lord, mark iniquities,
>   Lord, who can stand?
> But with you is forgiveness,
>   that you may be revered.
>
> I trust in the Lord;
>   my soul trusts in his word.
> More than sentinels wait for the dawn,
>   let Israel wait for the Lord.
>
> For with the Lord is kindness
>   and with him is plenteous redemption;
> And he will redeem Israel
>   from all their iniquities.

Intercessions: Offer intercessions for the church and the world. Use free, spontaneous intercessions; or use The Seven Offerings found in Appendix A; or at the beginning of the evening have group participants write down their prayer needs on a small piece of paper and place them in a bowl in the center of the group. At this time, members draw out one of the petitions and make a prayer of intercession. Then take the paper home and pray for your prayer partner all week.

The Lord's Prayer: Pray together the Our Father.

The Closing Prayer: Pray together a closing prayer from Appendix A.

The Closing Blessing

Leader: May the Lord bless us, protect us from evil,
        and bring us to everlasting life.

All: **Amen.**

Leader: Praise and Thanksgiving be evermore to Jesus!

All: Who with his blood has saved us.

All share a sign of peace.

9. You Will Be with Me in Paradise

Opening Prayer

Leader: In the name of the Father, and of the Son,
and of the Holy Spirit.

All: Amen.

Leader: O God, come to our assistance.

All: Lord, make haste to help us.

Leader: Glory to the Father, and to the Son,
and to the Holy Spirit.

**All: As it was in the beginning, is now,
and will be forever. Amen.**

Leader: Let us pray.

Almighty Father of our Lord Jesus Christ,
you sent your Son
to be born of woman and to die on a cross,
so that through the obedience of one   [one man]
estrangement might be dissolved for all.   [all men]

Guide our minds by his truth
and strengthen our lives by the example of his death,
that we may live in union with you
in the kingdom of your promise.

Grant this through Christ our Lord.

All: Amen.

The Gospel Text Is Read

■ Luke 22:14–23:56

When the hour arrived, Jesus took his place at table, and the apostles with him. He said to them: "I have greatly desired to eat this Passover with you before I suffer. I tell you, I will not eat again until it is fulfilled in the kingdom of God."

Then taking a cup he offered a blessing in thanks and said: "Take this and divide it among you; I tell you, from now on I will not drink of the fruit of the vine until the coming of the reign of God."

Then taking bread and giving thanks, he broke it and gave it to them, saying: "This is my body to be given up for you. Do this as a remembrance of me." He did the same with the cup after eating, saying as he did so: "This cup is the new convenant in my blood, which will be shed for you.

"And yet the hand of my betrayer is with me at this table. The Son of Man is following out his appointed course, but woe to that man by whom he is betrayed." Then they began to dispute among themselves as to which of them would do such a deed.

A dispute arose among them about who would be regarded as the greatest. He said: "Earthly kings lord it over their people. Those who exercise authority over them are called their benefactors. Yet it cannot be that way with you. Let the greater among you be as the junior, the leader as the servant. Who, in fact, is the greater—he who reclines at table or he who serves the meal? Is it not the one who reclines at table? Yet I am in your midst as the one who serves you. You are the ones who have stood loyally by me in my temptations. I for my part assign to you the dominion my Father has assigned to me. In my kingdom, you will eat and drink at my table, and you will sit on thrones judging the twelve tribes of Israel.

"Simon, Simon! Remember that Satan has asked for you to sift you all like wheat. But I have prayed for you that your faith may never fail. You in turn must strengthen your brothers." "Lord," he said to them, "at your side I am prepared to face imprisonment and death itself." Jesus replied, "I tell you, Peter, the rooster will not crow today until you have three times denied that you know me."

He asked them, "When I sent you on mission without purse or traveling bag or sandals, were you in need of anything?" "Not a thing," they replied. He said to them: "Now, however, the man who has a purse must carry it; the same with the traveling bag. And the man without a sword must sell his coat and buy one. It is written in Scripture,

'He was counted among the wicked,'

and this, I tell you, must come to be fulfilled in me. All that has to do with me approaches its climax." They said, "Lord, here are two swords!" He answered, "Enough."

Then he went out and made his way, as was his custom, to the Mount of Olives; his disciples accompanied him. On reaching the place he said to them, "Pray that you may not be put to the test." He withdrew from them about a stone's throw, then went down on his knees and prayed in these words: "Father, if it is your will, take this cup from me; yet not my will but yours be done." An angel then appeared to him from heaven to strengthen him. In his anguish he prayed with all the greater intensity, and his sweat became like drops of blood falling to the ground. Then he rose from prayer and came to his disciples, only to find them asleep, exhausted with grief. He said to them, "Why are you sleeping? Wake up, and pray that you may not be subjected to the trial."

While he was still speaking a crowd came, led by the man named Judas, one of the Twelve. He approached Jesus to embrace him. Jesus said to him, "Judas, would you betray the Son of Man with a kiss?" When the companions of Jesus saw what was going to happen, they said, "Lord, shall we use the sword?" One of them went so far as to strike the high priest's servant and cut off his right ear. Jesus said in answer to their question, "Enough!" Then he touched the ear and healed the man. But to those who had come out against him—the chief priests, the chiefs of the temple guard, and the ancients—Jesus said, "Am I a criminal that you come out after me armed with swords and clubs? When I was with you day after day in the temple you never raised a hand against me. But this is your hour—the triumph of darkness!"

They led him away under arrest and brought him to the house of the high priest, while Peter followed at a distance. Later they lighted a fire in the middle of the courtyard and were sitting beside it, and Peter sat among them. A servant girl saw him sitting in the light of the fire. She gazed at him intently, then said, "This man was with him." He denied the fact, saying "Woman, I do not know him." A little while later someone else saw him and said, "You are one of them too." But Peter said, "No, sir, not I!" About an hour after than another spoke more insistently: "This man was certainly with him, for he is a Galilean." Peter responded, "My friend, I do not know what you are talking about." At the very moment he was saying this, a rooster crowed. The Lord turned around and looked at Peter, and Peter remembered the word that the Lord had spoken to him, "Before the rooster crows today you will deny me three times." He went out and wept bitterly.

Meanwhile the men guarding Jesus amused themselves at his expense. They blindfolded him first, slapped him, and then taunted him: "Play the prophet; which one struck you?" And they directed many other insulting words at him.

At daybreak the council, which was made up of the elders of the people, the chief priests, and the scribes, assembled again. Once they had brought him before their council, they said, "Tell us, are you the Messiah?" He replied, "If I tell you, you will not believe me, and if I question you, you will not answer. This much only will I say: 'From now on, the Son of Man will have his seat at the right hand of the Power of God.'" "So you are the Son of God?" they asked in chorus. He answered, " It is you who say I am." They said, "What need have we of witnesses? We have heard it from his own mouth."

Then the entire assembly rose up and led him before Pilate. They started his prosecution by saying, "We found this man subverting our nation, opposing the payment of taxes to Caesar, and calling himself the Messiah, a king." Pilate asked him, "Are you the king of the Jews?" He answered, "That is your term." Pilate reported to the chief priests and the crowds, "I do not find a case against this man." But they insisted, "He stirs up the people by his teaching throughout the whole of Judea, from Galilee, where he began, to this very place." On hearing this Pilate asked if the man was a Galilean; and when he learned that he was under Herod's jurisdiction, he sent him to Herod, who also happened to be in Jerusalem at the time.

Herod was extremely pleased to see Jesus. From the reports about him he had wanted for a long time to see him, and he was hoping to see him work some miracle. He questioned Jesus at considerable length, but Jesus made no answer. The chief priests and scribes were at hand to accuse him vehemently. Herod and his guards then treated him with contempt and insult, after which they put a magnificent robe on him and sent him back to Pilate. Herod and Pilate, who had previously been set against each other, became friends from that day.

Pilate then called together the chief priests, the ruling class, and the people, and said to them: "You have brought this man before me as one who subverts the people. I have examined him in your presence and have no charge against him arising from your allegations. Neither has Herod, who therefore has sent him back to us; obviously this man has done nothing to deserve death. Therefore I mean to release him, once I have taught him a lesson." The whole crowd cried out, "Away with this man; release Barabbas for us!" This Barabbas had been thrown in prison for causing an uprising in the city, and for murder. Pilate addressed them again, for he wanted Jesus to be the one he released.

But they shouted back, "Crucify him, crucify him!" He said to them for the third time, "What wrong is this man guilty of? I have not discovered anything about him deserving the death penalty. I will therefore chastise him and release him." But they demanded with loud cries that he be crucified, and their shouts increased in violence. Pilate then decreed that what they demanded should be done. He released the one they asked for, who had been thrown in prison for insurrection and murder, and delivered Jesus up to their wishes.

As they led him away, they laid hold of one Simon the Cyrenean who was coming in from the fields. They put a crossbeam on Simon's shoulder for him to carry along behind Jesus. A great crowd of people followed him, including women who beat their breasts and lamented over him. Jesus turned to them and said: "Daughters of Jerusalem, do not weep for me. Weep for yourselves and for your children. The days are coming when they will say, 'Happy are the sterile, the wombs that never bore and the breasts that never nursed.' Then they will begin saying to the mountains, 'Fall on us,' and to the hills, 'Cover us.' If they do these things in the green wood, what will happen in the dry?"

Two others who were criminals were led along with him to be crucified. **When they came to Skull Place, as it was called, they crucified him there, and the criminals as well, one on his right and the other on his left. [Jesus said, "Father, forgive them; they do not know what they are doing."] They divided his garments, rolling dice for them.**

The people stood there watching, and the leaders kept jeering at him, saying, "He saved others; let him save himself if he is the Messiah of God, the chosen one." The soldiers also made fun of him, coming forward to offer him their sour wine and saying, "If you are the king of the Jews, save yourself." There was an inscription over his head:

"THIS IS THE KING OF THE JEWS."

One of the criminals hanging in crucifixion blasphemed him, "Aren't you the Messiah? Then save yourself and us." But the other one rebuked him: "Have you no fear of God, seeing you are under the same sentence? We deserve it, after all. We are only paying the price for what we've done, but this man has done nothing wrong." He then said, "Jesus, remember me when you enter upon your reign." And Jesus replied, "I assure you: this day you will be with me in paradise."

It was now around midday, and darkness came over the whole land until midafternoon with an eclipse of the sun. The curtain in the sanctuary was torn in two. Jesus uttered a loud cry and said,

"Father, into your hands I commend my spirit."

After he said this, he expired. The centurion, upon seeing what had happened, gave glory to God by saying, "Surely this was an innocent man." After the crowd assembled for this spectacle witnessed what had happened, they returned beating their breasts. All his friends and the women who had accompanied him from Galilee were standing at a distance watching everything.

There was a man named Joseph, an upright and holy member of the Sanhedrin, who had not been associated with their plan or their action. He was from Arimathea, a Jewish town, and he looked expectantly for the reign of God. This man approached Pilate with a request for Jesus' body. He took it down, wrapped it in fine linen, and laid it in a tomb hewn out of the rock, in which no one had yet been buried.

That was the day of Preparation, and the sabbath was about to begin. The women who had come with him from Galilee followed along behind. They saw the tomb and how his body was buried. Then they went back home to prepare spices and perfumes. They observed the sabbath as a day of rest, in accordance with the law.

Silence

Rest in the presence of what you have just heard, in the presence of Jesus, the living word of God. It is Jesus who is speaking in this passage, speaking to each one of us as individuals.

What does Jesus say? What does he say to you?

This is a time to listen—to listen anew if the passage is familiar. Jesus invites us to listen first with the ears of the heart. To help themselves listen with the ears of the heart, ancient Christians let a word or a short phrase, a single image, completely take hold of them. Let the word or phrase from the text choose you. Repeat it over and over, slowly in your mind and heart. This is not the time to ask theological questions or add anything to the text.

There are no right or wrong choices here. If a phrase does not come into focus after a bit of silence, begin reading the passage to yourself, taking your time. Stop whenever a phrase or image connects with you.

Keep things simple in this silence. Do not try to do too much work.

A Word or a Phrase

After the silence, members mention a word or phrase in the passage that appealed to them or spoke to them.

The Passage Is Read a Second Time

For the second reading, read only the section of the Gospel in bold.

Silence

In this silence you can do a little more work. This is the time to engage Jesus in a conversation. Ask him questions about what you heard. Go somewhere with that word or phrase you heard. Talk to Jesus about it. What did he mean? Why did he say this? What is he asking of you at this time? Occasionally in this silence, repeat the word or phrase from above, slowly, over and over again. Then go back to your part of the conversation. In this way, the word of God is always inserted into the conversation.

I See, I Hear, I Feel

After the silence, mention one thing you think the Lord may be saying to you.

Begin your statement with "I see," "I hear," or "I feel."

The Background Is Read

Luke's presentation of the passion gives us a different perspective on Jesus. The marginalized accompany Jesus on his journey—the women of Jerusalem, the good thief. Moved by the women's compassion, Jesus in turn consoles them. The hallmark of Jesus' attitude in this Gospel is "Father, forgive them." The presence of the Father and Jesus' intimate union with him are clear. Jesus assures the good thief, and us, that this day ends in paradise. Jesus trusts; God's faithfulness is never in doubt.

Also quite evident in Luke's passion story is the interplay between heaven and earth as the story progresses. Every moment, every detail has cosmic significance. In fact, for Luke the passion is the pivotal event in the history of the universe. Most of the characters are completely oblivious to the import of the events taking place around them. The disciples fail to see that the Passover they are sharing is the heavenly banquet itself brought down to earth. The Jewish leaders fail to see that Jesus is indeed the Messiah, God's anointed one, the Christ. Pilate and Herod both fail to see that Jesus really is king of the Jews. Even the crowds, both the ones crying, "Crucify him," and the ones who wailed in lament as Jesus went to the cross, fail to understand the hidden significance of what they are seeing. Luke's point, of course, is that we come to see the deeper significance of this story of stories.

The Gospel of Luke reminds us that those who suffer with and for others, who love with all their selfless hearts, are destined to be outside the walls of our society. Christianity is a call to walk that walk on a daily basis, to walk it "com-passionate-ly" with those outside society's walls, and it is also a call to break down those walls that separate us from the suffering, the marginalized.

Faith-Sharing: Individual and Group Process

See pages 8–9 for instructions.

- As you hear Luke's passion account this time, with what character do you identify most closely? (Among the characters to consider: Jesus, Peter, Judas, Pilate, Herod, the good thief, Barabbas, the lamenting women, Simon of Cyrene, the centurion, Joseph of Arimathea, onlookers, crowd demanding Jesus' execution.) What experience connects you to this character?

- As you reflect on Luke's passion account, in what ways do you identify with Jesus? Here are some possible points of connection:

  - a friend pledged to stand by you in a time of difficulty but couldn't handle it when you really needed him or her

  - you decided to accept a struggle that you could not avoid

  - you had to deal with an important decision or challenge when everyone close to you seemed unable to pay attention to what you were going through or were focused on unimportant things

  - people close to you tried to help you or defend you in ways that contradicted the principles by which you live

  - your words were turned against you or you were taunted when your dreams and hopes and plans looked foolish

  - a stranger understood you and appreciated you in unlikely circumstances

For personal reflection

Discerning an Action Response

What invitations and challenges do you hear? Consider your relationships with members of your family, your friends, people you work with, and those you encounter in your everyday activities. Whom do you need to treat differently? What are you, your family, and your small group called to do? Be sure to select action responses that you can actually begin to carry out.

Here are some more concrete questions and ideas that may help you focus your desire to respond to this Gospel.

- Recall the character in the Gospel passage with whom you identify the most. Think of how your life connects with this character's. Share this connection in a conversation with Jesus and the character in your prayer during the week. If you wish to explore the Gospel from another perspective, choose one or more other characters in the story.

- If you have not participated in the sacrament of reconciliation recently, attend a reconciliation service or go to confession before Holy Thursday in preparation for celebrating Easter.

- Celebrate the paschal Triduum—Holy Thursday, Good Friday, and the Easter Vigil—with your parish community and at home in new ways. Here are some suggestions:

  - Come to the Easter Vigil, or part of it, if this is not your family's usual practice.

- Make the Holy Thursday collection for the poor a richer experience by contributing money saved by eating simple meals at home during Holy Week.

- Invite grandparents and older members of the family to share their memories of Good Friday and Easter celebrations in church and at home. Pray together after family meals.

- Set aside some time to keep watch on Saturday in the midst of Easter preparations, or attend morning and midday prayer if your parish celebrates them.

Closing

Invitation to Prayer

Leader: Come, Holy Spirit, fill the hearts of your faithful.

All: Kindle in us the fire of your love.

Leader: Send forth your Spirit and we shall be created.

All: And you shall renew the face of the earth.

The Psalm (from Psalm 22)

Antiphon: My God, my God, why have you abandoned me?

> All who see me scoff at me;
>   they mock me with parted lips, they wag their heads:
> "He relied on the Lord; let him deliver him,
>   let him rescue him, if he loves him."
>
> Indeed, many dogs surround me,
>   a pack of evildoers closes in upon me;
> They have pierced my hands and my feet;
>   I can count all my bones.
>
> They divide my garments among them,
>   and for my vesture they cast lots.
> But you, O Lord, be not far from me;
>   O my help, hasten to aid me.

> I will proclaim your name to my brethren;
>> in the midst of the assembly I will praise you:
> "You who fear the Lord, praise him;
>> all you descendants of Jacob, give glory to him."

Intercessions: Offer intercessions for the church and the world. Use free, spontaneous intercessions; or use The Seven Offerings found in Appendix A; or at the beginning of the evening have group participants write down their prayer needs on a small piece of paper and place them in a bowl in the center of the group. At this time, members draw out one of the petitions and make a prayer of intercession. Then take the paper home and pray for your prayer partner all week.

The Lord's Prayer: Pray together the Our Father.

The Closing Prayer: Pray together a closing prayer from Appendix A.

The Closing Blessing

Leader: May the Lord bless us, protect us from evil,
and bring us to everlasting life.

All: **Amen.**

Leader: Praise and Thanksgiving be evermore to Jesus!

All: **Who with his blood has saved us.**

All share a sign of peace.

Appendix A: Prayers

Closing Prayer

Lord, we are your people,
draw us close to you.
Heal the broken-hearted,
touch those who are in pain,
Call back those who have strayed,
Warm hearts that have grown cold.

Help us to know your love
Through Jesus and through the Spirit.
Help us to spread that love and
Show it to everyone.
Help us to build love on justice and
justice on love.
Help us to believe mightily,
Hope joyfully, Love divinely.
RENEW the Spirit in us, so that we may help
RENEW the face of the earth.

Amen.

Prayer to Mary

Mary, you are a woman wrapped in silence
and yet the Word born of your yes
continues to bring life to all creation.
Mary, help us to say yes—
to be bearers of good news to a world waiting.
Mary, you are virgin and a mother
empowered by the Holy Spirit.
Help us to open ourselves
to that same life bringing Spirit.

Mary, help us to say our yes.
Mary, you are gift of Jesus to us,
Mother of the church.
Look upon the world and our lives.
Pray for us to your Son
that we might be renewed
that we may help renew the face of the earth.
Mary, help us to say yes.

Amen.

Prayer for Children

Lord, we love you very much.
Let us understand your love for us.

Your love for us flows
throughout the world.

God says I will call back
those who have strayed.

Let us stay close to you
every moment of our life.

Amen.

God of Mercy

God of mercy and compassion,
we thank you for drawing near to us in Jesus
and making us your children.

Continue to transform us
so that we can show
your love, compassion, and justice
to all people.

Renew your Spirit in us,
so that we may help renew the face of the earth.

Amen.

God of Love

God of love and mercy,
we rejoice in your presence among us.

Make our homes and our parish
sources of peace, generosity, and welcome.

We know that you delight in us
when we make your presence known
in our daily lives.

Renew your Spirit in us,
so that we may help renew the face of the earth.

God of Goodness

God of infinite goodness,
we thank you for your gifts to us.

Most of all, we thank you for sending Jesus to us
so that we may know your love, mercy,
    and compassion.

Form us into a parish family
that reaches out to embrace
all who are seeking.

Help us to reflect your desire
that all people find life in you.

Renew your Spirit in us,
so that we may help renew the face of the earth.

The Seven Offerings

All: **Loving God, we offer you the Precious Blood of Jesus, poured out on the cross and offered daily on the altar, for the glory of your name, for the coming of your kingdom, for the salvation of all people.**

Leader: Praise and thanksgiving be evermore to Jesus.

All: **Who with his Blood has saved us.**

Leader: Glory be to the Father, and to the Son,
and to the Holy Spirit.

All: **As it was in the beginning, is now,
and will be forever. Amen.**

All: **Loving God, we offer you the Precious Blood of Jesus,
poured out on the cross and offered daily on the altar,
for the spread of the church,
for all those consecrated to you by baptism,
for sisters, brothers, deacons, priests, and bishops,
for our bishop and for Pope John Paul,
and for the sanctification of all the people of God.**

Leader: Praise and thanksgiving be evermore to Jesus.

All: **Who with his Blood has saved us.**

Leader: Glory be to the Father, and to the Son,
and to the Holy Spirit.

All: **As it was in the beginning, is now,
and will be forever. Amen.**

All: **Loving God, we offer you the Precious Blood of Jesus,
poured out on the cross and offered daily on the altar,
for the conversion of every heart,
for the loving acceptance of your word,
and for the union of all Christians.**

Leader: Praise and thanksgiving be evermore to Jesus.

All: **Who with his Blood has saved us.**

Leader: Glory be to the Father, and to the Son,
and to the Holy Spirit.

All: **As it was in the beginning, is now,
and will be forever. Amen.**

All: **Loving God, we offer you the Precious Blood of Jesus,
poured out on the cross and offered daily on the altar,
for our civil authorities,
for the strengthening of public morals,
that life may be respected from conception**

to natural death,
and for peace and justice among all nations.

Leader: Praise and thanksgiving be evermore to Jesus.

All: **Who with his Blood has saved us.**

Leader: Glory be to the Father, and to the Son,
and to the Holy Spirit.

All: **As it was in the beginning, is now,**
and will be forever. Amen.

All: **Loving God, we offer you the Precious Blood of Jesus,**
poured out on the cross and offered daily on the altar,
for the sanctification of our work and our suffering,
for the poor, the sick, the afflicted,
and for all who rely on our prayers.

Leader: Praise and thanksgiving be evermore to Jesus.

All: **Who with his Blood has saved us.**

Leader: Glory be to the Father, and to the Son,
and to the Holy Spirit.

All: **As it was in the beginning, is now,**
and will be forever. Amen.

All: **Loving God, we offer you the Precious Blood of Jesus,**
poured out on the cross and offered daily on the altar,
for our own special needs both spiritual and temporal,
for those of our relatives, friends and benefactors,
and also for those of our enemies.

Leader: Praise and thanksgiving be evermore to Jesus.

All: **Who with his Blood has saved us.**

Leader: Glory be to the Father, and to the Son,
and to the Holy Spirit.

All: **As it was in the beginning, is now,**
and will be forever. Amen.

All: **Loving God, we offer you the Precious Blood of Jesus,
poured out on the cross and offered daily on the altar,
for those who are to die this day,
for all who have gone before us marked with the sign
of faith,
for those whose faith is known to you alone,
and for our final union with Christ in glory.**

Leader: Praise and thanksgiving be evermore to Jesus.

All: **Who with his Blood has saved us.**

Leader: Glory be to the Father, and to the Son,
and to the Holy Spirit.

All: **As it was in the beginning, is now,
and will be forever. Amen.**

Appendix B:
Suggested Reading from the Catechism

Suggested Background Material
from the Catechism of the Catholic Church

This material is selected both to complement the Gospels and to enable families to join in the three years of preparation for the Jubilee Year 2000. Throughout 1998, the Holy Father has asked us to reflect on the Holy Spirit and the Spirit's presence in the community. The role of the Holy Spirit in the life of Jesus and in the church is an important theme in the Gospel of Luke, proclaimed in year C.

Paragraph numbers are given so that these suggestions can be used with any edition of the *Catechism*. (The page numbers vary from edition to edition, but the paragraph numbers are always the same.)

March 1, 1998

535–540: The Spirit and Jesus' baptism, temptations, and the inauguration of his ministry

March 8, 1998

702–730: God's word and Spirit at work

March 15, 1998

733–741: Bearing fruit in the power of the Spirit

March 22, 1998

976–987: "I believe in the forgiveness of sins"
1468–1470: The effects of the sacrament of reconciliation

March 29, 1998

1422–1448: The sacrament of reconciliation

April 5, 1998

727–730: The mission of the Son and the Holy Spirit
606–628: Christ offers himself to the Father; the *Catechism*'s reflections on the passion

More Resources for Faith Sharing

LORD YOU MUST BE JOKING
Bible Stories That Tell Your Story

Eugene Webb

Paper, 176 pages, 5.5" x 8.5"   Leader's Guide: Paper, 80 pages, 5.5" x 8.5"

People remember stories. And that's what you get in this great resource from family therapist Eugene Webb. Great stories, set into a biblical context — with a twist that makes you think — about the story, about the bible, about your story. Reflection questions help the process. A companion leader's guide helps you use the stories in retreats for adults or youth — or as a supplemental activity in family and other group situations.

WHY SMALL CHRISTIAN COMMUNITIES WORK

Msgr. Timothy O'Brien

Paperbound, 64 pages, 5.5" x 8.5"

The key to forming Christians is forming small communities. In a small Christian community, says Msgr. Timothy O'Brien, you can't be anonymous. You have to share your faith — and relate to others. This little book is essential reading for all newly formed faith-sharing groups or anyone contemplating forming such a group. Bulk prices available.

DEEPDOWN SPIRITUALITY
Seasonal Stories That Invite Faith-Sharing

Joseph J. Juknialis

Paper, 192 pages, 5.5" x 8.5"

Joseph J. Juknialis, a popular and imaginative storyteller, has turned his hand to real-life personal stories that work especially well for faith-sharing groups. Topical and seasonal indices help you select the right story for the right time. This is a collection of poetic/prose reflections on the Sunday Scriptures throughtout the three cycles of the lectionary.

Order these books from your local bookseller or call: CODE: L1
1-888-273-7782 (toll free) or 1-408-286-8505
or visit the web site at www.rpinet.com